WHEN HE CALLS YOU
by Name

**BECOMING THE PERSON
GOD CREATED YOU TO BE**

KERRY JOHNSTON

www.HopeForTransformation.com

This book is dedicated to
Carla, Rhonda, Melissa, and Andrew

✳ ✦ ✳

Mighty Warrior Press
Austin, Texas
www.HopeForTransformation.com

Cover and interior design by TLC Graphics, www.TLCGraphics.com
Cover: Tamara Dever; Interior: Monica Thomas

Unless otherwise noted, scripture references are taken from THE HOLY BIBLE, NEW INTERNATIONAL VERSION®, NIV® Copyright © 1973, 1978, 1984, 2011 by Biblica, Inc.® Used by permission. All rights reserved worldwide.

Others quoted are marked (NLT) *The Holy Bible, New Living Translation,* copyright © 1996, 2004, 2007 by Tyndale House Foundation, used by permission of Tyndale House Publishers, Inc., Carol Stream, Illinois 60188; (Amplified) *The Amplified® Bible,* copyright © 1954, 1958, 1962, 1964, 1965, 1987 by The Lockman Foundation (www.Lockman.org); (NKJV) *The New King James Version®,* copyright © 1982 by Thomas Nelson, Inc.; (NET) (New English Translation) *NET Bible®,* copyright © 1996–2006 by Biblical Studies Press, L.L.C. http://netbible.com; (Modern Language) *The Modern Language Bible: The New Berkeley Version in Modern English,* copyright © 1945, 1959, 1969 by Zondervan Publishing House; (The Message) *The Message,* copyright © 1993, 1994, 1995, 1996, 2000, 2001, 2002, used by permission of NavPress Publishing Group; (NASB) *The New American Standard Bible®,* copyright © 1960, 1962, 1963, 1968, 1971, 1972, 1973, 1975, 1977, 1995 by The Lockman Foundation; (English Standard Version) *The ESV® Bible (The Holy Bible, English Standard Version®),* copyright © 2001 by Crossway, a publishing ministry of Good News Publishers. Used by permission. All rights reserved.

ISBN 978-0-692-25013-6
LCCN 2014912297
Printed in the United States of America

CONTENTS

INTRODUCTION

Something about human beings is unique in all creation. It is the ability to see beyond our present circumstances, to reach beyond our grasp, to strive for more. We have an innate desire to become what we are not yet. Maybe the best way to say it is that we have hope.

I would like to have an atheist explain to me where his hope comes from, because the only possible source of hope I can see is God. I can't come up with any other logical explanation for the hope that lies within us.

Our language is replete with phrases that encourage us to move forward: Dream big. Go for it. Be all you can be. Yet our circumstances seem to bring a natural resistance to hope. The daily grind of life. Lack of funds. Loneliness and discouragement. Illness. The stuff that just happens.

If it is true that God is the source of hope, then it would be logical that Satan is the source of discouragement. That makes sense to me.

It is pretty evident that there is a war going on. Satan is our mortal enemy. He is working overtime to mess up our lives.

He has been doing this for a long time, and he is really good at it. Satan is the consummate liar, murderer, and thief. Jesus said, "The thief [Satan] comes only to steal and kill and destroy; I have come that they may have life, and have it to the full." (John 10:10) That's the good news. Even in this fallen world, Jesus offers us a life different from the one available to most people. It's an abundant life. If we understand that, we can lay hold of it.

Remember in the movie *Bambi* when the young fawn ventured onto the frozen pond? He tried and tried to stand up, only to fall down again each time. Finally he went spinning out of control across the ice. The only thing that saved him was that he eventually got to solid ground.

That's a pretty good picture of my life. Lots of spinning out of control. Lots of falling down and getting back up. A desperate need for solid ground.

Two things make it hard to get up from our collective fall. One is that Satan constantly works to keep the ice slippery. The other is that it happened in the Garden of Eden centuries before we were born. Eden is a place we've never seen. We have no memory of how it *should* be. But God does.

The Bible tells us that a great life is within our reach. But we have settled for less. I'm convinced that deep down in our heart of hearts, we know it. There is an ache for more—a divine discontent. We long for the abundant life Jesus promised.

How do we lay hold of abundant life? That is a question only God can answer, and the answer will be different for each of us.

Think about it. God created us. He made each of us for a purpose. He who knows the end from the beginning knows what our lives are supposed to accomplish.

God knows the person He created us to be. If we can find out who we are and why He put us here, we are well on our way to the abundant life He wants us to have.

God knows our true name. When He calls us by name, the path to our destiny opens. But can we hear Him say it? We have to in order to accept His purpose for our lives and to step into all He has for us.

That's what this book is about.

SECTION ONE

ENCOUNTER

CHAPTER 1

A ROCK IN MY SHOE

Elijah was a man just like us.

JAMES 5:17

*T*he last thing Satan wants us to have on earth is the kind of life Jesus promised. That's because an abundant life is the most powerful evangelistic tool there is. When our life is filled with joy and purpose, it attracts people whose lives are not. They are drawn to us because we have something they want.

Lies are Satan's number one weapon against us. If he can get us to believe his lies about the blessings God wants us to have, he can cut us off from the fullness of life God wants us to enjoy. Without meaning to, we begin to cooperate with Satan. We live small lives that cause our Christian witness to be diminished.

That's how I lived in my early Christian years. Perhaps you can identify with my struggles.

A Rock in My Shoe

It doesn't make a lot of sense to walk with a rock in your shoe. As soon as you take a step or two and realize it's there, you might as well stop wherever you are and get rid of it. Until you do it's not going to get any better. Most of the time it will only get worse.

But wait. Imagine you are in a marching band, and your band is marching in a major televised parade. Things are going swimmingly until the band member in front of you kicks up a small stone and—zip—it goes right into your shoe as if it had eyes and loved Keds®. Now the problem takes on a whole new life. This is your band's moment in the sun. Would you rather ruin it or walk with a rock in your shoe?

Let's pursue this line of thought a little further. Suppose you live in a society where people have always had rocks in their shoes. Each day you feel the pain and see the grimaces. Each night you see the damage. Still, every morning when you get dressed you dutifully take the rock off the dresser and place it in whatever pair of shoes you are wearing that day. Why? Because everybody does it. Because it has been done this way for generations. Because your leaders keep telling you that's the way it's supposed to be. And because they tell you that on some great and wonderful day in the future you will go to heaven and all rocks will be removed from all shoes forever.

Sounds a little silly, I know. Yet, for years I tried to live a rock-in-my-shoe type of Christianity. I want to say I didn't know better, but that's not exactly right. Deep down, I knew something was wrong, but I didn't fully understand what it was. And while the pain ebbed and flowed, it never completely went away.

Stories from the Bible

Frankly, a lot of the pain had to do with the stories I read in the Bible. Take the disciples, for example. They got to live, converse, and interact with Jesus. Talk about Christianity made easy. Surely I could have faith, do great ministry, and see miraculous power flow through me if only God would appear directly to me, assure me of His caring existence, and tell me exactly what to do with my life.

But no—I lived under a new covenant that was somehow supposed to be better than all that. I had been given the Bible, and that was all I needed. I had the opportunity to study the Bible and learn about what God used to do, what He had done for me, and what He was going to do someday in the future. In the meantime, I could be good, go to church, and tell others about what a great life I had. I was supposed to be happy with that.

And I almost was, except for that little bit of rock-in-my-shoe pain.

If my pain were to ever have a name, it probably would have been Elijah. He got to hear from God and go tell the king of Israel what God had said. Elijah got to pray prayers that mattered, prayers that brought drought and then, three-and-a-half years later, rain.

Elijah was fed by ravens and by angels. He stayed with a widow and ate from her food jars that never went empty. He defeated the prophets of Baal in an amazing demonstration of the power of God. He outran a chariot and traveled 40 days and 40 nights without food or water. Finally, Elijah stood on the mountain of God and witnessed the glorious approach of God's presence, then heard His audible, small, still voice.

Never mind that he had a hard life and was often in danger of being killed. Elijah lived—I mean *really* lived—and then he passed his mantle on to Elisha before being taken up into heaven in a fiery chariot. Elijah exemplified powerful, God-directed living. He made a difference and, well...I didn't. Compared to Elijah, I felt like a fish in a sandstorm. So I struggled with nagging questions. How was life without miracles better than life with them? Why did I live with a constant feeling that something was missing in my Christian experience?

One scripture in particular bothered me. It almost seemed as if God had tucked it into the New Testament just to torment me. It rang true neither to my experience nor to what I had been taught. Yet there it was, challenging me, haunting me, refusing to go away. "Elijah was a man just like us." (James 5:17, NIV, 1995)

I had been taught—either directly or by inference—that Elijah was not at all like us. He—and the other men of the Bible whom I envied—fell into a special category for one of two reasons. Either they occupied a special office, such as that of a prophet or apostle, or they lived in a special time or dispensation, such as the Exodus, the life of Jesus, or the age in which the church was established.

Two things were painfully obvious to me: I did not occupy a special office, and I did not live in a special time. I wanted to ask God why he had different rules for different people. I wanted to know how, under the new covenant, my normal was better than their normal. For many years it seemed as if the only answer I received was, "Elijah was a man just like us."

THE CRUX OF THE MATTER

Either Elijah was just like us or he wasn't. Either the new covenant is better than the old covenant or it isn't. The Bible says one thing, but we have behaved as if the opposite were true. All the while it seems as if Christians are content to limp along, trying to meet the minimum requirements for getting to heaven.

Maybe it's time to take off that shoe, remove the rock, examine it, and ask one simple question: Why is it in there?

* * *

CHAPTER TWO

THE MIDDLE of NOWHERE

I have called you by name; you are mine.

ISAIAH 43:1, NLT

*G*ideon was living with way less than the abundance God wanted him to have. Fortunately, God intervened. His intervention changed not only Gideon's life, but the course of the nation of Israel. We can learn a lot from Gideon's story.

LIVING WITH THE ENEMY

Gideon blinked against the sweat, dirt, and chaff assaulting his face. The by-products of threshing wheat only added misery to its boredom. But Gideon's mind was not really in the moment. His thoughts kept going back to the problem of the Midianites. He paused and shook his head.

The Midianites were a curse upon his family and the people of Israel. "Whenever the Israelites planted their crops, the Midianites, Amalekites, and other eastern peoples invaded the country. They camped on the land and ruined the crops all the way to Gaza and did not spare a living thing for Israel, neither sheep, nor cattle, nor donkeys. They came up…like swarms of locusts. It was impossible to count them or their camels; they invaded the land to ravage it." (Judges 6:3-5)

For seven years the eastern tribes ebbed and flowed through Israel like tsunamis, driven by deep hatred and leaving nothing but destruction in their wake. When they left, the dread of them stayed behind. There was no question they would be back. Impoverished and dejected, the Israelites cried out to the Lord for deliverance.

In response, the Lord sent a prophet to His people. He reminded them that the Lord had told them not to follow the gods of the Amorites, whose land He had given them. Then He added, "But you have not listened to me." (Judges 6:10) God had spoken, but the people had not paid attention. Now they were facing the consequences.

Israel's plight weighed heavily on Gideon's mind. He looked up to the hills where dens were prepared in which he and his loved ones would hide when the enemy returned. His gaze moved sadly down the slopes to the cluster of buildings his family called home.

That's when he saw the messenger.

Gideon's body tensed. Giving the man his full attention, he edged toward his sword propped against the winepress wall. Tension hung in the air like the moment between lightning and thunder. One more step and Gideon would reach for his weapon.

The stranger stopped. He sat down. Gideon relaxed a little.

The messenger looked Gideon in the eye. Finally, he spoke. "The Lord is with you, mighty warrior." (Judges 6:12)

Seven words to change a man's life. Seven words to alter the course of a nation.

Gideon turned to face the man squarely. He felt anything but mighty. And surely no hero would thresh his wheat in a winepress to conceal it from his enemies. *Mighty warrior.* Gideon could hardly believe his ears. He saw himself as the weakest member of the smallest clan in the tribe of Manasseh. (Judges 6:15) Gideon was sure he had been born into insignificance. He felt too small to even be on the map.

The messenger had come to set this right. His words were carefully chosen. They were the exact words Gideon needed to hear.

IDENTITY THEFT

Gideon didn't know who he was. He had fallen victim to identity theft, but not the modern kind involving stolen credit cards or social security numbers. This was much worse. Satan had taken from Gideon the very understanding of whom God had created him to be. Without that knowledge, Gideon was incapable of becoming the person God intended. He could only stumble blindly down a path that would never lead him to his destiny.

Having no hope and no future, Gideon had settled for survival. Because Gideon perceived himself as weak and insignificant, he hadn't even considered facing his enemies. Seeking neither victory nor defeat, Gideon had refused to engage in battle. Instead of standing with a bloody sword, he had settled for the short end of the stick.

ABANDONED

Gideon, no doubt, had been one of the Israelites calling out to the Lord for deliverance. Gazing up at the stranger, Gideon wondered whether or not this might be God's answer to his prayers. Clearly, it wasn't the answer he expected.

The Lord is with you. The stranger's words and Gideon's reality did not match up. One can sense Gideon's frustration in his reply to the visitor. "If the Lord is with us, why has all this happened to us? Where are all his wonders that our fathers told us about when they said, 'Did not the Lord bring us up out of Egypt?' But now the Lord has abandoned us and given us into the hand of Midian." (Judges 6:13)

For Gideon, there could be no other explanation. God had packed up and moved out. And now that the Lion had departed, the Midianite jackals were free to move in.

WHERE ARE ALL HIS WONDERS?

Gideon could recount the miraculous signs God performed when He delivered Israel from Egyptian slavery. He knew by heart the stories of God's supernatural provision for His people in the wilderness. He had also been told about God's promise to his forefather, Abraham, assuring him that through his off-spring every nation of the world would be blessed. But Gideon drew no comfort from these facts. There was no apparent connection between his circumstances and his head-knowledge of God's power and promises. Gideon found himself hopelessly stuck between what God had done for His people in the past and what He would do for them in the future.

Many Christians are living in Gideon's dilemma. We hold in our hands the Bible, bearing witness to God's miracles long ago. We have in our heads the promise of heaven through the redemptive work of Christ. But nothing stirs in our hearts. We find ourselves stuck in the middle of nowhere, an empty desert between what God has done in the past and what He will do in the future. In the meantime, life consists of trying to plod on dutifully, if not joyfully, without any expectation of seeing God move in our generation.

Without the hope of God's active involvement in our lives, it appears we have come to believe that "God's kingdom will come either by death or by the rapture, but in the meantime all we can do is endure as gallantly as possible with no hope of God's will ever being done on earth…. What a terrible way to live!'"[1]

ASSUMPTIONS

A woman stepped into an airport shop and purchased a newspaper and a small package of cookies. Since she had a few minutes before her flight, she found a seat and began to read the front page. After a while she heard a crackling sound. Glancing to her side, she caught a glimpse of someone's hand reaching out and taking one of her cookies. Not wanting a confrontation, she ceremoniously took a cookie, too, hoping to establish her ownership of the goodies. The offender failed to get the message. Another cookie disappeared; then another. Finally, only one cookie remained. To her amazement, the audacious thief took the last cookie, broke it in two, and offered her half. She sat speechless, quietly stewing until the attendant announced her flight. Only when she opened her purse to get her boarding pass did she discover her unopened cookies tucked snugly on top of her wallet.[2]

Fortunately for the woman in the story, her wrong assumption left her with only a moment of embarrassment and a

---

1   Ed Silvoso, *Anointed for Business* (Ventura, CA: Regal Books, 2002), p. 106.

2   Craig Brian Larson, *Illustrations for Teaching and Preaching* (Grand Rapids, MI: Baker Book House, 1993), p. 9.

good story to tell. Our incorrect assumptions about God's involvement in our lives are much more costly. They keep us from God's purposes. They cause us to accept lives that are too small. They leave us stuck in the middle of nowhere.

*H*OPING FOR HEAVEN

Our understanding of God's commitment to the present is vital. If He is not available to us in our current circumstances, we have little to hope for besides heaven. We sit like rusty old cars in the rain waiting for God to come back and fix us up.

Salvation is a precious gift, but our future in glory has little impact on the crisis we face today. The idea of someday reaching heaven doesn't deliver the answer to the prayer we prayed last night. It doesn't instill hope for living a life that makes a difference. It's too far in the future.

In the meantime, we have settled for getting by. Such living is predictably joyless, selfish, and random. Without a greater purpose we just exist. We function, but we do not truly live.

*U*NBELIEF

Has God abandoned the land? No one in the church of my youth ever came right out and said it, but the idea was expressed in a teaching that went something like this: God sent His Son to die in order to save us from our sins. After Christ ascended into heaven, God sent the Holy Spirit. The Spirit helped get the early church established and inspired the apostles to write the New Testament. But since we presently have the Bible in its entirety, God has nothing else to say. And since He has provided for our salvation, there isn't much left for Him to do, either. So, He quietly sits far away in heaven, waiting for the proper moment for Jesus to return and take us home.

At first blush, this sounds sort of true. The Bible is the complete and inspired word of God. Since nothing can be added to it or subtracted from it, God must not have anything more to say. And if the Word equips us for every good work, then there shouldn't be anything left for the Holy Spirit to do, either. The life we are experiencing is as good as it gets. All we need to do is attend church once a week/month/year to remind God we're still signed up for our fire policy from The Afterlife Insurance Company (Motto: For a good life it's Afterlife). In essence we are saying, "Lord, we still want heaven, but other than that, we expect nothing." This is a subtle but devastating form of unbelief.

NOT ABANDONED

The Bible resonates with a different truth: We are *not* abandoned. "For He [God] Himself has said, 'I will not in any way fail you *nor* give you up *nor* leave you without support. [I will] not, [I will] not, [I will] not in any degree leave you helpless *nor* forsake *nor* let [you] down (relax My hold on you)! [Assuredly not!].'" (Hebrews 13:5, Amplified)

The idea that God has somehow "checked out" is a significant and successful lie straight from the mouth of Satan. He has perpetrated it upon God's people for so long that it has become the rock we voluntarily put into our shoes each day.

We have accepted an orphan spirit.

The cry of God's heart is for His people. "I will give them a heart to know me, that I am the Lord. They will be my people, and I will be their God, for they will return to me with all their heart." (Jeremiah 24:7)

Christianity is about having a heart-to-heart relationship with God. If we lose heart, we lose everything. From our heart comes our true identity.[3]

Life should not consist of struggling with the art of behavior management. Life is what comes from inside you when you are truly alive.

"We have no idea who we really are.... We thought this whole Christian thing was about ... trying not to sin. Going to church. Being nice."[4] This "best behavior religion" offers the appearance of righteousness without the fruit of righteousness. It offers the hope of someday going to heaven while killing the hope of living a life that matters in the meantime.

Jesus was way more than the nicest guy ever. He was holy. And, he was powerful.[5]

Jesus came to earth to make a difference. He didn't come just to die. He came to show us how to live.

Jesus has much more in store for us than being good little soldiers left to occupy the earth until He returns. If we are to be like Him, we must fully live. We were created to have an impact.

Imagine how good it would feel to live like that.

God's word came to Gideon at just the right time to transform him from wimp to warrior. It awakened something way down in Gideon's heart that gave him hope for meaningful change. "The desire for transformation lies deep in every human heart.... The possibility of transformation is the essence of hope."[6]

---

3   John Eldredge, *The Journey of Desire* (Nashville, TN: Thomas Nelson Publishers, 2000), p. 2.

4   John Eldredge, *Waking the Dead* (Nashville, TN: Thomas Nelson Publishing, 2003), p. 80.

5   Eldredge, *The Journey of Desire,* p. 54.

6   Ortberg, *The Life You've Always Wanted,* p. 20.

Like Gideon, we cannot change without a word from God. We need God to tell us who we are. He holds the key to our destinies.

$\mathcal{T}$HE PLANS I HAVE FOR YOU

There is a being in this universe who wants us to settle for average lives, but it is not God.[7] Our Father never for one moment wanted us to live with a survival mentality. "'For I know the plans I have for you,' declares the Lord, 'plans to prosper you and not to harm you, plans to give you hope and a future.'" (Jeremiah 29:11)

God formed each of us uniquely for reasons He had in mind before the beginning of time. God had an individual purpose for us in our creation, and He has personal intentions for us in His redemption.[8] Satan knows this and fights it with all his might. One of Satan's greatest victories has been to turn Christianity into a game we play in our heads rather than a reality we live from our hearts.

When God promises a future, He is not talking about one so distant that we lose heart waiting for it. Finding our identity in Him is the key to our destiny. "It is there…that confidence can be found and secured, establishing certainty about who we are, what we are destined to become, and what God has called us to do."[9]

Could you be open to the possibility that God might have a greater purpose for regular people like you and me? "Or will you settle with the view that these are just quiet days for

---

7 Ortberg, *The Life You've Always Wanted*, p. 64.

8 Jack Hayford, *Grounds for Living* (Tonbridge, Kent, England: Sovereign World Ltd., 2001), p. 58.

9 Jack Hayford, *Grounds for Living*, p. 12.

the church—days to muddle through, somehow to survive, to hope for the best?"[10]

Gideon saw himself as incapable of making a difference, but the Lord went to great lengths to convince him otherwise. (Judges 6:15-16) God does not want us to be afraid to fight. He has already won the battle on our behalf, but we must still engage the enemy. The only way Satan can win is by convincing us not to confront him.

Peace at the price of our destiny is not peace at all. It is defeat.

We must accept God's plan for our lives, not Satan's. Only our Father can turn our paltry sticks into swords.

* ⁜ *

10   Terry Virgo, *Men of Destiny* (Eastbourne, E Sussex, England: Kingsway Publications Ltd), p.93.

CHAPTER 3

IS THE LORD AMONG US?

If we don't change the direction we are going,
we may end up where we are headed.

CHINESE PROVERB

ℛUBBER DUCKS

Every year thousands of merchant ships sail from ports around the world, their decks stacked with colorful tractor-trailer-sized shipping containers. These ocean-going pack mules move 95 percent of the world's cargo. The containers they carry hold everything from motorcycles to mascara.

The United States alone receives some 500 million of these boxes annually. Considering the number that must be shipped worldwide, it should come as no surprise that about 10,000 of them are lost into the ocean each year.

In 1992 a ship lost some of its cargo during a Pacific storm. One container—holding 29,000 rubber ducks and other floating bath toys such as turtles and frogs—broke open, releasing its contents into the churning sea. The ducks and their buoyant friends thus began an impromptu migration through the world's oceans.

By 2001 the squeaky toys had floated north through the icy Bering Strait and reached the North Atlantic waters near the site where the *Titanic* went down. From there a portion of the toys continued eastward toward Europe, while others headed south, bound for the East Coast of America. Some may still be adrift, thousands of miles from their point of release. Powered by nothing but wind, waves, and ocean currents, these tiny vagabonds have shown oceanographers much about the behavior of the ocean's surface. They also serve as a colorful reminder that plans do sometimes go "afowl."[1]

(D)RIFTING

Imagine a bright yellow-and-red rubber duck, whose entire world was supposed to consist of one bathtub, cast adrift in the vast Pacific Ocean. Once intended to be a sudsy shipmate in Shallowater, Texas, or a bathtub buddy in Birmingham, Alabama, our little duckling is now floating west of Alaska, with no legs or webbed feet and only useless, painted-on wings. Incapable of going anywhere under its own power, it will be carried wherever the wind and the ocean currents please. Originally meant to be seen and enjoyed by innocent eyes and squeezed by tiny hands, it now provides only a temporary diversion for a seagull.

God created each of us to contribute something unique and wonderful to this world, but if we don't know what that something is, we might as well be lost rubber ducks, doing nothing, changing nothing, and going nowhere in particular. If we are not moving toward our destinies with purpose and power, there are plenty of currents in this world to move us,

---

1   Byran Nelson, http://www.mnn.com/earth-matters/wilderness-resources/stories/
what-can-28000-rubber-duckies-lost-at-sea-teach-us-about-our-oceans? March 11, 2011.

but there is no telling where we may end up or what we may look like when we get there.

Gideon never made a conscious decision to live in the middle of nowhere. He didn't wake up one day and say, "My life is too good. I think I'll see how badly I can mess it up."

Instead, he wound up in the middle of nowhere the same way we did—without meaning to. Gideon allowed himself to be carried there by a powerful spiritual force. Adrift in life with no sense of identity or destiny, he found himself propelled into misery by the subtle but strong current of his culture.

We are subject to the same kinds of forces. From the moment we are born, Satan uses our culture to subtly weave his lies into the fabric of our lives. Some of the things I learned and came to accept as true were the things that caused me to walk a rock-in-my-shoe Christianity.

Sadly, our culture is the worst place from which to learn what is true and what is not.

Think about what is glorified in American culture. The list would include money, sex, knowledge, power, success, sports, and technology. Spiritual life would be lucky to make the top ten. Let's face it: Most Americans put their hope in one or more of these things rather than in God.

Here's the problem with money, knowledge, and the other things listed above. None of them cares one bit that we exist. They are not aware of us in any way. They have no plans for us. None of them can really make us happy, and none of them can show us our destinies.

AWARENESS

Most of the indoctrination we receive and accept from our culture—that thing most people would call our worldview—is taken in between the ages of 18 months and 13 years. Charles Colson calls it the gospel of health, wealth, and success. If there is any room for God in our thinking, we often see Him as the God of the gaps. We perceive that we need God only to fill the needs that pleasure, money, and success do not.[2]

One of the reasons this indoctrination is such a useful tool for the enemy is that we are unaware the process is taking place. If we ever do wake up to it, we are behind from the get-go. It takes a lot of work to replace Satan's ingrained lies with God's honest truth.

Awareness is kind of a strange commodity. Some things, like loud noises, demand our attention. There are other things we choose to be aware of. For example, whenever I buy a new car, I suddenly begin to notice every car like mine on the road. I have invested in that car, it has value to me, and so I notice others like it. Mostly we pay attention to the things that are important to us and that align with our priorities.

Genesis tells the story of Jacob's flight from Beersheba to Haran. Jacob had left town in a hurry to avoid the wrath of his brother, whose birthright he had just stolen. When he could go no farther, Jacob stopped to spend the night.

While sleeping, he saw a vision in which the Lord appeared to him and renewed the covenant He had made with his father, Abraham. Afterward, Jacob named the place Bethel and confessed, "Surely the Lord is in this place, and I was not aware of it." (Genesis 28:16)

We cannot afford to live out our lives unaware of God's presence. He never intended for our first encounter with Him to be at the gates of heaven. What a tragedy it would be for Him to confront us with words like these: "I was there, but

---

2   Charles Colson, *Kingdoms in Conflict* (William Morrow and Zondervan Publishing House, 1987), p. 220.

you were not looking for Me. I was in this place, and that place, and at this point I wanted to move in your life, but you were not aware of Me, so you missed it. Why was it so difficult to get you to pay attention?"

How would we answer God?

Remember, we always pay attention to one thing at the cost of ignoring something else. We choose what to be aware of and what not to. The fact that it is our choice means it is also our responsibility. We will someday be held accountable for it.

Gideon lived in a culture a lot like ours. The Israelites doubted that their God even cared for them. They doubted whether He was near.

God took exception to this attitude. He would later send His prophet to declare, "They have lied about the Lord; they said, 'He will do nothing!'" (Jeremiah 5:12)

Jesus also confronted this lie. "My father is always at his work to this very day." (John 5:17) God is still active, but somehow we have lost the joy of being aware of it. If we question God's availability, we will eventually come to ignore Him. If we doubt that He cares for us, we will always turn to other gods.

𝒯ROUBLE IN THE WILDERNESS

The Israelites had no excuse for not being aware of God's presence. After they had endured some 400 years of slavery in Egypt, God moved mightily on His people's behalf. He set them free with an awesome display of His power in a series of plagues and mighty miracles which Gideon referred to as "His wonders." Yet, in spite of everything God did on their behalf, the Israelites failed to connect with their powerful God.

From the moment they left Egypt, the Israelites struggled with the presence of the Lord. This happened even though

He stayed with them constantly in the form of cloud or fire: "By day the Lord went ahead of them in a pillar of cloud to guide them on their way, and by night in a pillar of fire to give them light, so that they could travel by day or night. Neither the pillar of cloud by day nor the pillar of fire by night left its place in front of the people." (Exodus 13:21-22)

Still, the people doubted. When it looked like the Egyptian army would trap them beside the Red Sea, they sarcastically asked Moses, "Was it because there were no graves in Egypt that you brought us to the desert to die?" (Exodus 14:11)

Later, water became the issue. At Rephidim Moses struck a rock, which produced water for the people to drink, but not before Israel again questioned, "Why did you bring us up out of Egypt to make us and our children and our livestock die of thirst? … Is the Lord among us or not?" (Exodus 17:3, 7)

Finally, the children of Israel asked Aaron to make them a golden calf to worship. They did so in spite of all the things the Lord had done on their behalf. But there is a simple explanation for their unfaithfulness. The people had already forgotten why God had set them free.

cA FEAST IN THE WILDERNESS

Let my people go. Most everyone remembers Moses and Aaron's famous imperative to Pharaoh. They actually had a good bit more than that to say.

"Thus says the Lord God of Israel: 'Let My people go, that they may hold a feast to Me in the wilderness.'

"And Pharaoh said, 'Who is the Lord, that I should obey His voice to let Israel go? I do not know the Lord, nor will I let Israel go.'

"So they said, 'The God of the Hebrews has met with us. Please let us go three days' journey into the desert and sacrifice to the Lord our God, lest He fall upon us with pestilence or with the sword.'" (Exodus 5:1-3, NKJV)

As Americans, we take pride in our freedoms. But we tend to forget that our freedoms are limited by the Constitution and by the laws of the land. We don't have the absolute freedom to do whatever we want—there *are* limits.

It was the same with Israel. In fact, God spelled out exactly why He wanted to set them free: so they could honor Him with a festival and offer sacrifices in the desert. In other words, God liberated Israel for one purpose—so they could worship Him.

But the Israelites were like us. They wanted the freedom to do whatever they pleased. This caused them to mishandle the presence of the Lord.

The Fear of the Lord

Before Moses ascended Mount Sinai to receive the law from God, the people could see the glory of the Lord on the mountain. This marked a pivotal moment in the history of Israel:

> When the people saw the thunder and lightning and heard the trumpet and saw the mountain in smoke, they trembled with fear. They stayed at a distance and said to Moses, "Speak to us yourself and we will listen. But do not have God speak to us, or we will die."
>
> Moses said to the people, "Do not be afraid. God has come to test you, so that the fear of God will be with you to keep you from sinning."

The people remained at a distance, while Moses approached the thick darkness where God was. (Exodus 20: 18-21)

How did God's presence test the people of Israel? The answer is in Moses' seemingly contradictory statement to them. Moses told them not be afraid, but to fear the Lord. He spoke of two different kinds of fear. The first makes us afraid of God, causing us to draw back from Him out of a desire for self-preservation. The second is a reverent fear that pulls us toward God and is willing to risk anything to experience the awe of His majestic presence.

God tested the Israelites to find out what kind of fear they would display. His intent was to reveal whether the Israelites would choose to be afraid of Him and keep their distance, or to draw near Him in reverence and awe, experiencing His splendor and majesty in a way that would cause them to walk in obedience.

The people chose to stay away. This must have crushed God's heart. He had declared His purpose for Israel only a few days earlier: "You yourselves have seen what I did to Egypt, and how I carried you on eagles' wings and brought you to myself." (Exodus 19:4)

God wanted to bring His people into His presence and dwell among them like a father. "I thought to myself, 'I would love to treat you as my own children!' I wanted nothing more than to give you this beautiful land—the finest possession in the world. I looked forward to you calling me, 'Father,' and I wanted you never to turn from me." (Jeremiah 3:19, NLT)

God is a personal God. His heart's desire is to bring us to Him. We cannot come close to God without worshipping Him, and we cannot worship Him without drawing near.

That's the reason God created man in the first place. Worship is what we were made for.

But the people told Moses, "Speak to us yourself and we will listen. But do not have God speak to us, or we will die." They failed to see God as central. They wanted secondhand religion. Because they were afraid to die, they never found out how to live.[3]

ℱINDING OUT HOW TO LIVE

Our culture has also taught us to be afraid of God. It has presented God as an angry old man who only wants to punish us. It has instilled in us a fear of hearing God's voice, telling us we have to be crazy to do so. The truth is we should be much more afraid of being *without* God than we are of being near Him.[4] Without the presence of God, freedom is an empty waste—a wilderness.

God is not an angry taskmaster out to vaporize us for making the slightest mistake. He wants to help us be better, not catch us doing something wrong. He wants to empower us, not bind us with rules and regulations. If all God wanted from us was behavior modification, He could accomplish that with a cattle prod.

The children of Israel drew back from God because of the selfish orientation of their hearts. They wanted what they wanted, not what God wanted. From the start they had not been satisfied with God's provision for them. They constantly complained and asked for something different or something

---

3 Major W. Ian Thomas, *The Saving Life of Christ and The Mystery of Godliness* (Grand Rapids, MI: Zondervan Publishing House, 1988), p. 150.

4 John Bevere, Sermon, title unknown, Gateway Church, May 2, 2004.

more. They were even willing to turn away and worship an idol in the hope that it would give them what they wanted.

The Bible minces no words in condemning their decision. "For although they knew God, they neither glorified him as God nor gave thanks to him, but their thinking became futile and their foolish hearts were darkened. Although they claimed to be wise, they became fools and exchanged the glory of the immortal God for images made to look like mortal man and birds and animals and reptiles." (Romans 1:21-23)

The Israelites traded the glory of God for the golden image of a calf. They were afraid that if they turned fully to God, He might ask more of them than they were willing to give. So they chose a smaller god which allowed them to maintain control of their own lives. In doing so, they became fools.

We have the ability to choose what we will become. It all depends on whom or what we choose as our god.

God invites us to approach Him in godly fear—to find our destinies in worship. Wisdom draws us toward God to worship; fear makes us run away and hide.

Unfortunately, staying away from God always leads to unbelief. If we keep God at a distance, we are not able to believe He is close enough to help us when we need Him.

Faith is difficult because it requires us to trust God more than we trust what we see with our eyes. The Israelites were unwilling to take the difficult road of trust. As soon as things started looking bad, they began to complain. They were more attuned to their circumstances than to their God.

Oftentimes, so are we. We become so tuned in to what is going on around us that we forget something is supposed to be going on within us. We become so distracted, rushed, pre-occupied, or fearful that we settle for a mediocre version of our faith. Our thinking becomes futile. We live on the surface rather than going deep with God. We end up skimming our lives instead of actually living them.[5]

The Beginning of Wisdom

"The fear of the Lord is the beginning of wisdom, and knowledge of the Holy One is understanding." (Proverbs 9:10) By being afraid of God, the children of Israel cut themselves off from wisdom. From that point forward they were doomed to stumble on in the dark wisdom of the world, making one bad decision after another.

One generation missed out on the opportunity to enter the Promised Land. The next failed to obey God by not completely destroying the land's inhabitants. Subsequent generations looked to the Canaanites for wisdom, falling deeper and deeper into the trap of idolatry.

This kind of thinking produced the cultural morass in which Gideon lived. The people wanted the benefits of living in the Promised Land without the cost of being totally sold out to God. Without relationship with the God who created them, they were capable of knowing neither who they were nor God's purposes for their lives. They became conditioned not to rely on God. Yet, when things went sour, they blamed the Lord for deserting them. But God had not abandoned the Israelites; the Israelites had abandoned God.

A Balloon Ride Gone Bad

John Ortberg once took a hot-air balloon ride while on vacation in California. He and his wife were joined on the flight

---

5   Ortberg, *The Life You've Always Wanted,* p. 77.

by another couple. As the couples introduced themselves, John told them he was a pastor.

Soon the balloon was airborne and a spectacular view opened up beneath them. But the euphoria didn't last. The walls of the basket were not nearly high enough. The pilot was a young man who didn't inspire a lot of confidence. Then he admitted it was his first time to pilot this type of balloon and that the landing might be a little rough. The pleasure ride took on the atmosphere of impending disaster.

Finally, the woman from the other couple spoke up. Looking at John, she said, "Do something religious."[6] She didn't know God or anything about pleasing Him or calling on His name. But she figured the pastor could handle it for her. After all, that was his job.

That's the way lots of Christians look at it. Their job is to go to church. The pastor's job is to hear from the Lord, conduct the services, pray, visit the sick, and do all that other religious stuff, so they don't have to. After all, *he's* the one who went to seminary. He gets paid. Let him take care of it.

We have repeated the foolishness of the Israelites. In effect, we have said to our leaders, "Speak to us yourselves and we will listen. But do not have God speak to us, or we will die." So we go to church once a week to see if God has anything to say. Unfortunately for those who want to live this way, going to church does not make you a Christian any more than getting in the water makes you a great white shark.

There is no such thing as vicarious salvation. We cannot slip into heaven on our pastor's coattails, reeking of the world and hoping we did just barely enough to be saved.

----

6   John Ortberg, *If You Want to Walk on Water You've Got to Get Out of the Boat* (Grand Rapids, MI: Zondervan, 2001), p. 12.

Without a direct relationship with God, we will always turn to other lovers.[7] When we are casual in our approach to God, everyone does what is right in his own eyes. Then only a strong leader can unite us. "Without a deep and burning desire of our own, we will be ruled by the desire of others."[8]

THE CREATION STORY

What if God were that casual about us? Here's what creation could have looked like.

In the beginning, God created everything. He created the light and separated it from the darkness. He thought about making some stars and planets, but it was getting late and He wanted to watch *Monday Night Football*. So He called it a day.

The next morning, He separated the land from the water. He thought about making beautiful mountains and valleys, deserts and rainforests, and rivers and lakes. Then He thought, "You know, most people are going to live here less than a hundred years. It really doesn't matter much what things look like, as long as the earth is functional." So He made everything look like eastern New Mexico and said, "That's good enough."

Later He made some blackbirds to fly in the sky, and some halibut for the oceans, and cats to walk on the dry land. He thought about making a host of other wonderful animals, but He was a little stressed out, so He went home and sat out on the patio.

By the end of the week God decided He was finished. Heading for His recliner, He turned back for one last look at everything He had made, and it wasn't too bad. He was

---

7   John Eldridge, *Wild at Heart* (Nashville, TN: Thomas Nelson Inc. 2001), p. 172.

8   Eldridge, *The Journey of Desire,* p. 62.

a little burned out by now, so He thanked Himself it was Friday and took the weekend off.[9]

*W*ORTHY OF *O*UR *W*ORSHIP

Of course, this is absolutely unthinkable. God did not create the middle of nowhere. He is not the one who put us into a powerless, lame-duck existence. Instead, He paid a great price to set us free, to get us out of our self-imposed prisons, and to bring us to Himself.

God does things with His entire being. That same God breathed Himself into us in the act of creation. He gave all of Himself for us in the act of redemption. He has promised He will never, never abandon us.

It is not too much to ask that we give Him our attention, awareness, and love — our worship — in return.

Worship is giving God our entire being, not just church attendance or being good. It is thinking about Him during the day and being humbled by His goodness, grace, and faithfulness. We have been offered the privilege of knowing Him and centering our entire existence on Him. Let's determine today to move in His direction. His presence is as far from the middle of nowhere as we can get.

*K*NOWING *G*OD *B*ETTER

Gideon went through several significant steps in finding and fulfilling his destiny. There are no shortcuts on the road to ours. The first, and most important, thing that happened to Gideon was that he came to know God in a better and more personal way. The messenger opened the door for Gideon's metamorphosis, but the significant change came after he went away:

---

9   Ortberg, *The Life You've Always Wanted*, p. 62.

And the angel of the Lord disappeared. When Gideon realized that it was the angel of the Lord, he exclaimed, "Alas, Sovereign Lord! I have seen the angel of the Lord face to face!"

But the Lord said to him, "Peace! Do not be afraid. You are not going to die." (Judges 6: 21-23)

Even after the angel of the Lord disappeared, Gideon could still hear God's voice. The angel's visit changed Gideon from someone who had information about God that had been passed on to him from others, to someone who knew God and was beginning to understand His character. Gideon came into a new way of knowing God based on personal relationship.

Each person's journey with God starts with some kind of encounter with Him. For Gideon it was a visit from a divine messenger. For Moses it was the burning bush. For Jacob it happened at Bethel, where he became aware of God's presence. For each it was a place of meeting with the Lord and beginning to know Him in a real and personal way. If we cannot encounter God, we have no hope of living a life that matters.

KNOWING HOPE

Only after Gideon heard God was he ready to tear down his father's idols. (Judges 6:25-27) Once we have encountered the true and living God, we realize the emptiness of all lesser gods and the foolishness of placing our trust in any other. Hearing His voice increases our faith, changes our priorities, and allows us to orient our lives around Him.

It is not enough just to tear down our idols. God instructed Gideon to build "a proper kind of altar" in their place. (Judges 6:26) Without the proper kind of altar our worship will be neither acceptable nor powerful. Only the right kind of worship can change us.

Worship produces hope. Genuine hope in God brings an expectation that He might actually do something. The result is new boldness and determination to obey God and trust Him for the results. We move toward our destinies when we have a mandate from the Father.

*R*ETAKING OUR INHERITANCE

The angel Gideon encountered told him to "Go and save Israel." Following God always involves risk. God's calling drew Gideon into a great adventure. He was caught up in the midst of a dangerous story. As God's soldier and warrior, he was following Him into battle.[10]

It was a battle for Gideon's inheritance. Gideon was no longer content to occupy the Promised Land without enjoying the promises that came with it. Canaan was his by divine birthright, and he was ready to face the Midianites or anyone else who dared try to make it otherwise.

*A*PPREHENDING THE POWER OF GOD

Gideon, in his discouragement, asked the angel of the Lord, "Where are all his wonders?" He had heard of God's great power but had not seen it in operation in his lifetime. But Gideon's obedience opened the way for the power of God to bring victory. Gideon's sword became "a sword for the Lord." (Judges 7:20)

In the second book of Timothy, the apostle Paul warns Timothy about terrible times that will come in the last days. Among other things, he warns that people will love money and be proud, abusive, ungrateful, and unholy. The long list

---

10   Eldridge, *Waking the Dead,* p. 95.

concludes by saying people will "act religious, but they will reject the power that could make them godly." (2 Timothy 3:4-5, NLT)

Notice that he does not say people will deny the power of God. We all know God is powerful; that is part of what makes Him God. The problem comes, rather, from the rejection of the power of God for our own lives.

God cannot be God without His power, and we cannot be godly without it, either.

Just as a toaster cannot operate unless it has a power source, we cannot function as Christians if we are unplugged from God. Our lack of power actually comes from a failure to properly love God (verse 4). We lack power because we have lost connection with our Source.

Paul's Prayer for the Ephesians

There is a direct comparison to be drawn between Gideon's story and the apostle Paul's prayer for the church in Ephesus:

> I keep asking that the God of our Lord Jesus Christ, the glorious Father, may give you the Spirit of wisdom and revelation, so that you may know him better. I pray that the eyes of your heart may be enlightened in order that you may know the hope to which he has called you, the riches of his glorious inheritance in his holy people, and his incomparably great power for us who believe. (Ephesians 1:17-19a)

There are four components to Paul's prayer for the Ephesians:

+ That they might know God better through the Spirit of wisdom and revelation.

+ That they might know the hope to which He has called us.

+ That they might know the riches of His glorious inheritance in the saints.

+ That they might know the incomparably great power of God.

*L*EAVING NOWHERE

It is no coincidence that these are the same four areas in which Gideon had to overcome to fulfill his destiny. Satan is no fool. He knows where to attack us to cause us to live in defeat. Satan's methods were effective against Gideon, they posed a threat to the early church, and they have robbed much of the church of her destiny today.

Paul's prayer shows us how to counter Satan's schemes. To leave the middle of nowhere, we have to be willing to take a journey with God—to venture into new territory.

Recently I got on an airplane and took a seat not far from a little girl who was flying for the first time. Boarding took a while and several minutes passed. Finally, I heard her ask, "Are we flying yet?"

If someone has never flown, they can't know exactly what it is like. It may be the same for us as we step into a deeper relationship with God. We may feel uncertain and uncomfortable. There may even be some fear involved. But getting to our destination is worth the risk.

I am convinced God wants to stir up hope in our hearts to move us forward. We can recover the lost art of worship. We are perfectly capable of encountering our powerful God in a way that makes a difference today. If we open our eyes and ears, He will show us the way.

* \+ *

CHAPTER 4

GOD STILL SPEAKS

For if you are silent, I might as well give up and die.

PSALM 28:1, NLT

J have argued that God has a destiny for each of us, that our identity opens the way to our destiny, and that only God can tell us who we are and what that destiny is. In doing so I have made two assumptions that absolutely have to be correct for these things to be possible. The first is that God still speaks. The second is that each one of us is capable of hearing His voice.

These are significant assumptions. But, as the scripture above so clearly states, King David believed death was preferable to silence from God. "I pray to you, O Lord my rock. Do not turn a deaf ear to me. For if you are silent, I might as well give up and die." (Psalm 28:1, NLT)

The worst thing God can do to us is leave us alone.

God Listens

David touched upon the deep-seated fear in each of us that God will turn a deaf ear to our prayers. If God does not listen, He will not respond.

This is not the basis for an abundant life.

Picture David's prayer, accompanied by incense, moistened with tears, rising into heaven. As it approaches the throne of God, we see that the throne is empty. On the seat rests a large piece of cardboard with a hastily inscribed message in black marker: "Gone fishing. No prayers will be heard today."

That will never happen. The Bible lists only two legitimate reasons for unanswered prayer. "Yet you don't have what you want because you don't ask God for it. And even when you ask, you don't get it because your motives are all wrong—you want only what will give you pleasure." (James 4:2, NLT)

The only prayers God will not hear are the ones Satan talks us out of praying. The only prayers God will hear and not answer are carnal—prayed for the fulfillment of our own selfish desires.

Our prayer life reveals what we believe about God. If we see Him as distant and disconnected, our prayers will be half-hearted and shallow. If we perceive that He is loving and accessible, our prayer life will come alive.

*G*OD SPEAKS

David understood that silence from God offers nothing but a life not worth living. Silence is ground zero in the middle of nowhere. We will remain there under house arrest as long as we assume God no longer speaks.

Why have so many Christians given up on hearing His voice?

In the first place, there appear to be some pretty good reasons for not believing God speaks today. Some people insist that anyone who claims to hear from God is crazy. It doesn't help that there are people suffering from mental illness who claim they hear strange things from God. In the worst-case scenario, they even claim God told them to kill someone. If they carry out this "command" and it all eventually goes to a court of law, everyone pretty much agrees they are not right in the head because they claim to have "heard" God.

This is not a new problem. No one heard from God more clearly than Jesus. Yet, at one point in Jesus' ministry His own family "went to take charge of him, for they said, 'He is out of his mind.'" (Mark 3:21) Later, when Paul spoke about the resurrection of the dead to Agrippa, the king's response was, "You are out of your mind, Paul.... Your great learning is driving you insane." (Acts 26:24)

There are plenty of things about Christianity that do not seem to be sane. It doesn't make sense to lay down your life for someone else. It's not reasonable to say there is an unseen world that is more real than the world we see. (2 Corinthians 4:18) It isn't sane to hear an inaudible voice.

We should never be surprised if people think us strange or even a little bit crazy. In fact, we should probably be concerned if they don't. As Paul said, "If I were still trying to please people, I would not be a servant of Christ." (Galatians 1:10) However, to address the specific example above, no one could hear the Lord tell them to murder someone, because the Lord would never tell them to do something contrary to His written word. That person heard some other voice and wrongly believed it was God.

REAL PROBLEMS

The issue is misusing or misunderstanding the gifts of God. People have been wounded by the abuse, embarrassed by the faking, turned off by the grandstanding, and appalled at the insanity of some who claim to have heard from God. These are legitimate and maddening concerns. They cause real problems.

One night early in my career as a firefighter, my crew responded to a severe automobile accident. We arrived on the scene to find the aftermath of a head-on collision. A drunk driver had swerved across the road and struck another vehicle occupied by two teenaged girls. Both girls were seriously injured. In fact, in spite of our efforts, they both died. Two beautiful young women had their lives cut short by the folly of one impaired driver. It is an unpleasant memory that I still think about from time to time some 30 years later.

People misuse automobiles. Every day there are cars on the road driven by people who are inattentive, irresponsible, impaired, or insane. These folks cause accidents that kill and injure tens of thousands of people each year. But no one argues that we should stop using cars. In fact, it is difficult to visualize life without them.

In the same way, "ignorance, error, or folly is not an argument against the biblically valid experience of hearing the voice of God."[1] If we let the fear of misuse stifle the gifts God offers the church, we rob ourselves of life as He intended for us to have it.

*C*AN'T GET OUR MINDS AROUND IT

A second reason not to believe is that we are a society founded on logic and reason, and Christianity is not reasonable. It deals with the nebulous area of the spiritual, which cannot be scientifically studied. Therefore, it must all be hocus-pocus, myth, and fairy tale.

---

1   Jack Hayford, *Living the Spirit Formed Life* (Ventura, CA: Regal Books, 2001), p.27.

I've never quite been able to understand this line of thought. Love cannot be scientifically proved. It cannot be weighed, measured, or poured into a test tube for chemical analysis. Still, there are not a lot of people saying it doesn't exist.

People have an innate spiritual dimension. Deep inside we know there is more to our existence than what we experience in this lifetime. Eternity is somehow part of our make-up. That's because God "has also set eternity in the human heart." (Ecclesiastes 3:11)

Only God's voice can speak to the eternity within us. "For the message of the cross is foolishness to those who are perishing, but to us who are being saved it is the power of God. For it is written: 'I will destroy the wisdom of the wise; the intelligence of the intelligent I will frustrate.'" (1 Corinthians 1:18-19)

It's Already Been Said

There is a third reason not to believe God still speaks today. As mentioned in chapter two, many argue that since the Bible is God's full, final, and complete word, He cannot have anything else to say. This assumption seems all the more reasonable because it may line up with what we have been taught and what we have experienced.

Suppose for a moment that you married someone exactly three years ago today. Those first three years were a fairly normal, wonderful, and perplexing experience of sharing your new lives together and enjoying the intimacy of marriage. Every evening during those three years your spouse spent quite a bit of time writing in a diary, but you didn't think much about it.

However, on this your third anniversary your spouse brings the diary to you and gives you some startling news. Beginning today, the rules of your marriage change and your spouse will never speak to you again. You can still speak to him or her, but from now on your spouse will only refer to the diary and point to the relevant pages, basing every present and future experience on what is in the book.

Stunned, you walk outside and see the most beautiful sunset you could ever imagine. You excitedly run into the house and encourage your spouse to come see it. To your great disappointment, he or she is too busy to be interested. Quickly turning to chapter 22, verse 7, of the diary, your spouse points out that you shared a sunset on October 23. Been there, done that. Also see chapter 15 on busyness.

A tremendous sense of loss washes over you. You feel alone and abandoned. Why? Because every sunset is different. Each one offers a different kind of beauty and evokes a different emotional response that needs to be shared as part of a living, growing relationship. But under the new rules, none of this is possible. There can be only isolation and stagnation. Nothing will ever be the same.

Is that your idea of a relationship? Of course not. Nor is it God's.

Silence is the death of relationship.

Yes, God has spoken to us through His written word, the Bible. It was inspired of God and given to its writers by the Holy Spirit. It is the final authority on all matters of doctrine and ultimate truth. Nothing God will ever say to us will contradict it. So let's hear what the Bible has to say about this issue.

My Sheep Hear My Voice

In the tenth chapter of John, Jesus uses the analogy of the shepherd and the sheep. Calling himself "the good shepherd," He describes His relationship to the sheep: "The gatekeeper opens the gate for him, and the sheep listen to his voice. He calls his own sheep by name and leads them out. When he has brought out all his own, he goes on ahead of them, and his sheep follow him because they know his voice." (John 10:3-4)

Clearly, Jesus is saying that He has a voice and that His voice can be heard by His sheep. Was Jesus talking only about the period of time during which He was on the earth? No, because He goes on to say, "I have other sheep that are not of this sheep pen. I must bring them also. They too will listen to my voice, and there shall be one flock and one shepherd." (John 10:16) Jesus was referring here to the Gentiles, who would not be brought into the flock until after His ascension. Even after leaving the earth, Jesus has a voice that can be heard by His sheep.

But there is more. The passage says He calls His own sheep by name. Shepherds spend a lot of time with their sheep. They get to know them and they give them names.

Nobody knows you better than Jesus. He has a name for you and He will call you by that name. He will tell you who you were created to be.

God didn't put the story of Gideon in the Bible to make us feel badly about how He used to relate to people in the past. He put it there to show us how life is supposed to work. Hearing Him is an essential part of following Him. His sheep hear His voice.

THEY WILL ALL KNOW ME

One of the central promises of the new covenant is this, "No longer will they teach their neighbor, or say to one another, 'Know the Lord,' because they will all know me, from the least of them to the greatest." (Jeremiah 31:34) We need to take the Bible at face value. We should expect whatever was available to someone in biblical times to be available to us. The Bible says we can know God.

I admire Winston Churchill. I have read about Winston Churchill and watched television programs about his life. I have read some of his great speeches. Even so, I can neither hear his voice nor have a relationship with him. It is impossible to know someone who is not there and who does not speak. God tells us we can know Him, not just know *about* Him. For this to be possible He has to be there, and He has to speak to us.

I WILL NEVER FORSAKE YOU

"For the Lord your God goes with you; he will never leave you nor forsake you." (Deuteronomy 31:8)

God's promise is that He will never forsake us. He wants to engage with us. He is willing and eager to give us His time and attention, and He provides the means for us to stay engaged with Him.

God wants to speak to us through His written word and through the internal voice of the Holy Spirit. The two will never be in conflict; rather, they are intended to complement each other. "If I were not grounded in the Word and only tried to hear God subjectively from the Spirit, I could be easily deceived. If I only tried to understand and obey the

Word without the Holy Spirit, I would be dry and lifeless."[2] We need the balance that comes from being grounded in the Word and able to hear His voice.

We Need Specifics

"Now an angel of the Lord said to Philip, 'Go south to the road—the desert road—that goes down from Jerusalem to Gaza.'" (Acts 8:26) God had a job for Philip, but he wasn't in the right place. So God sent him a message, "Go." When Philip obeyed, he encountered the Ethiopian eunuch and introduced him to Christ.

God had a plan for the gospel to go to Ethiopia. But He wanted Philip to participate in that plan. So, He sent an angel to speak to Philip. Not because Philip was special, but because he was available. He would hear and obey.

Go south to the road—the desert road. This reminds me of the language the Lord used in speaking to Gideon. "Take the second bull from your father's herd, the one seven years old." (Judges 6:25) God is a God who is fully engaged with His people. He knows us and our circumstances to the most minute detail. And He will communicate with those who will listen.

As precious as the Bible is, it does not give us the specific guidance we need for life's questions. Should I take that promotion and move to another city? Is this the person I am supposed to marry? What should I say to the person in front of me? Are they ready to hear?

---

2   Mary Forsythe, *A Glimpse of Grace* (Dallas, TX: Kingdom Living Press, 2002), pp. 195-196.

*T*HE POWER OF A WORD

On January 25, 1990, an Avianca Airlines Boeing 707 crashed into a hillside in Long Island, New York, killing 73 of the 158 people on board. Because of delays caused by fog, the airliner had been circling JFK Airport for 77 minutes. The plane crashed because it ran out of fuel.

Before the crash, the pilot repeatedly told air traffic control that his aircraft was low on fuel. Eventually, one controller asked how much longer the airplane could stay aloft. The pilot said "about five minutes" and was given permission to land. Unfortunately, wind shear caused the first landing to be aborted, and the engines flamed out before a second landing attempt could be made.

An investigation determined that the fatal error which ultimately doomed the flight was the pilot's failure to report that he had a fuel *emergency*. Because he never used this key word as called for by procedure, he was not given the priority treatment that could have averted the disaster.

*C*ALLED

As Christians, we have failed to grasp the significance of some really important words in the Bible. One of these is the word "called." Every Christian has a beginning point in his or her walk with Christ. Our journey began when, in one way or another, God called us.

Paul stated that calling people was the essence of his ministry. "Through Him we received grace and apostleship to call all the Gentiles to the obedience that comes from faith for his name's sake. And you also are among those Gentiles who are called to belong to Jesus Christ." (Romans 1:5-6)

We are called from one way of life to another. "And we know that God causes everything to work together for the good of those who love God and are called according to his purpose for them. For God knew his people in advance, and he chose them to become like his Son, so that his Son would be the firstborn among many brothers and sisters. And having chosen them, he called them to come to him. And having called them, he gave them right standing with himself. And having given them right standing, he gave them His glory." (Romans 8:28-30, NLT)

"For many are called, but few are chosen." (Matthew 22:14) Not everyone is listening. Anyone can study the Bible, but not everyone will hear His voice.[3]

In our day, we usually acknowledge this dynamic only for "special" people. We speak of someone being called to the ministry or called to the mission field. But the truth is that if you have truly been saved, it was in response to a call from God. He said something to you—perhaps through the Bible, through a minister or friend, or even in the quiet privacy of your own home—and you heard Him. You heard something beyond the words, and you heard it from God. Something deep inside you received the Word, and it produced a change in your heart—a response that resulted in your salvation.

The reason we are Christians is that God called us, and we heard Him. When we responded to His call, He gave us right standing with Himself. God gives us right standing so that we can come into His presence, not just in the future, but now. When we hear His voice and step out in obedience, He uses

---

3 Erwin Raphael McManus, *The Barbarian Way* (Nashville, TN: Thomas Nelson Inc., 2005), p. 84.

us to reveal His glory to others, giving them the opportunity to see and hear.

You are called according to His purpose. His purpose for you originated before the beginning of time. That means you have a name and a destiny that was in place before God said, "Let there be light."

*W*ORD

"Man shall not live on bread alone, but on every word that comes from the mouth of God." (Matthew 4:4) The word for "word" here is "rhema," which means "that which has been uttered by the living voice, something spoken, speech, or disclosure."

The spoken word of God is essential to daily Christian living. We are still capable of hearing this word today—the life-giving, life-sustaining, life-directing, living word God speaks to us every day. Jesus indicated we need this word as badly and as often as we need bread.

*W*ORDS FOR LIFE

Let's examine a few scriptures in the light of this insight. Each of these verses refers to the *rhema* word of God.

✦ "The Spirit gives life, the flesh counts for nothing. The words I have spoken to you—they are full of the Spirit and life." (John 6:63) The *rhema* word of God and the Holy Spirit are intrinsically linked. It is the Holy Spirit who breathes life into us through the spoken word of God.

✦ "Whoever belongs to God hears what God says." (John 8:47) Hearing God's *rhema* word is both a function and an evidence of belonging to God.

+ "While Peter was still speaking these words, the Holy Spirit came on all who heard the message." (Acts 10:44) Once again we see a link between the word of God and the presence and indwelling of the Holy Spirit.

+ "But what does it say? 'The word is near you; in your mouth and in your heart,' (that is, the word of faith which we preach)." (Romans 10:8, NKJV) The *rhema* word can be heard in our hearts as well as from someone's mouth.

+ "Consequently, faith comes from hearing the message, and the message is heard through the word about Christ." (Romans 10:17) Faith is a product of hearing the *rhema* word.

+ "Take the helmet of salvation and the sword of the Spirit, which is the word of God." (Ephesians 6:17) The *rhema* word gives us the weapon we need for going on the offensive in our spiritual lives.

+ "The Son is the radiance of God's glory and the exact representation of his being, sustaining all things by his powerful word." (Hebrews 1:3) The *rhema* word—not dark matter—sustains the universe. If God stopped speaking, the universe would fall apart. No wonder scientists can't figure it out.

ENOUGH OF THIS SILENCE

If we heard God at the moment we were saved, we can hear Him again and again. The Bible contains story after story of men and women who heard God in one way or another. They are examples for us. "Hearing God is not only to be normal, but also...an essential proof of belonging to God."[4]

Hearing God is a simple description of Christianity in its purest form. "A person's spirituality is the sum of their responses to what they believe to be the voice of God."[5]

---

4   McManus, *The Barbarian Way*, p.83.

5   Hayford, *Living the Spirit Formed Life,* p. 165.

Our ability to hear God is the basis of our relationship with Him, because we cannot have relationship without the give and take of conversation. Our ability to hear His voice will determine just how intimately we know Him.

Hearing God's voice is the key to the abundant life God meant for us to enjoy.

Eternal life starts now and expands in all directions. Jesus spoke "not primarily of duration, but quality [of] life that is absolutely wonderful and can never be diminished or stolen from you."[6] Fullness of life follows and is dependent upon hearing and following the shepherd.

Hearing God means we have the ability day by day to believe and obey. It means the difference between living a life enslaved to rules and regulations and living free to go with God into the midst of a great adventure.[7] It means the difference between living by cold, hard law and living in relationship with a warm and loving heavenly Father.

Does God speak to us through His Word, the Bible? Absolutely. In fact, hearing God's voice through the Bible is by far the way we will hear Him most often. We cannot hear the voice of God effectively unless "The preciousness and absolute authority of the Word of God is central to our life and tradition."[8]

Reading the Bible is also the best way to learn to hear Him in other ways, because the Bible teaches us what His voice sounds like. "He always speaks on the basis that we know, love, study, and search the scriptures."[9] We can also

---

6   Eldredge, *The Journey of Desire*, pp. 38-39.

7   Eldredge, *Waking the Dead*, p. 95.

8   Hayford, *Living the Spirit Formed Life*, p. 27.

9   Hayford, *Living the Spirit Formed Life*, p. 28.

place God's word into our hearts through listening to godly teaching, listening to Christian music, reading Christian books, and through prayer and meditation. Putting God's word in our hearts prepares us to hear Him. "The heart has become the new dwelling place of God, and it is in the heart that we hear his voice."[10]

To hear God, we must want to hear Him. We have to be willing to invest our time and energy toward hearing Him. We will never share the deep things of our hearts with those who do not care to listen. Neither will God.[11]

God has not abandoned us and He never will. He still speaks and He wants us to speak to Him, to converse with Him, to have communion with Him because He loves us and because every sunset is different.

Maybe we should stop living as if we were locked in a sound-proof booth. It's time to break the shell of disbelief that has isolated us from our heavenly Father. We desperately need an encounter with God—an encounter so real, powerful, and frightening that in the midst of it God has to assure us, "Peace. Do not be afraid. You are not going to die." God is still looking for those who will not shrink back from His presence like Israel did at Mount Sinai. The desire of His heart still is, as it was then, to bring us to Himself.

✳ ✢ ✳

---

10   Eldredge, *Waking the Dead,* p. 86.

11   John Bevere, *Drawing Near* (Nashville, TN: Thomas Nelson Inc., 2004), p. 145.

SECTION TWO

EMBRACE

CHAPTER 5

I WILL NEVER LEAVE YOU

And I will ask the Father, and he will give you another
advocate to help you and be with you forever — the Spirit of
truth.... You know him, for he lives with you and will be in you.
I will not leave you as orphans....

JOHN 14:16-18

Sizing Up and Downsizing

Gideon looked out over the army he had assembled, now camped by the spring of Harod. The men occupied themselves with sharpening their weapons and filling their animal-skins with water. It was still amazing to him how the Lord had taken him from threshing wheat in a winepress to being commander of an army of more than 32,000 men.

Gideon, like any good commander, had probably sent scouts to size up the opposition, camped not far away to the north. Their report, no doubt, confirmed what he suspected. His army was at a huge numerical disadvantage. Nevertheless, Gideon knew the Lord was on their side. With God's help, even Gideon's comparatively small army could win the upcoming battle.

Then the Lord told Gideon, "You have too many men for me to deliver Midian into their hands." (Judges 7:2, NIV, 1995) The Bible doesn't say what went through Gideon's mind at that moment, but I know what would have gone through mine: "I have what?"

Nevertheless, the Lord continued, "In order that Israel may not boast against me that her own strength has saved her, announce now to the people, 'Anyone who trembles with fear may turn back and leave Mount Gilead.' So twenty-two thousand men left, while ten thousand remained." (Judges 7:2-3, NIV, 1995)

Still, God wasn't finished. He pared down the army even more, all the way down to three hundred men. No way could the Israelites boast about their own strength now. They needed nothing less than a miracle.

And so it was. That night, when Gideon's three hundred men raised torches and sounded trumpets, God caused the Midianites to turn on each other with their swords. God gave the victory and deserved all the credit.

*L*ED BY THE SPIRIT

The Holy Spirit was vitally involved in Gideon's success. The Bible tells us, "Then the Spirit of the Lord came on Gideon." (Judges 6:34) The Holy Spirit was there, guiding and strengthening Gideon to accomplish the task God had given him to do. Perhaps that explains Gideon's calm when God reduced his army to next to nothing. He was operating in a state of empowered grace provided by the Holy Spirit Himself.

In Old Testament times, the Holy Spirit would temporarily "come upon" or "fall on" people, and they would do extraordinary things. Samson received his great strength in this way: "Then the Spirit of the Lord came powerfully upon him. He went down to Ashkelon [and] struck down thirty of their men." (Judges 14:19)

But the Holy Spirit did not indwell people in the Old Testament. Even while Jesus was with the disciples, He told them, "You know him [the Counselor, the Holy Spirit], for he lives with you and will be in you." (John 14:17) He was with them because He was in Jesus, but He would not be in them until the day of Pentecost, when they were baptized with the Holy Spirit. (Acts 1:5, Acts 2)

It Is for Your Good that I Am Going Away

Before Jesus' crucifixion, He bared His heart to the disciples (John 14-16). In that important moment Jesus spoke plain truths meant to sustain them during and after the traumatic events that were approaching. At one point He told the disciples, "I tell you the truth: It is for your good that I am going away." (John 16:7a, NIV, 1995) It is no wonder Jesus had to assure them He was telling the truth. What the Lord was saying was incomprehensible—He was leaving, and it was for the disciples' own good.

What could be better than Immanuel, God with us? Only one thing could possibly be better than Jesus, God with us: the Holy Spirit, God *in* us.

Jesus stated it plainly: "Unless I go away, the Counselor will not come to you." (John 16:7b, NIV, 1995) Jesus left in bodily form so that God could indwell men in the form of the Holy Spirit. The disciples would no longer see Jesus face to face; they would have fellowship with Him spirit to spirit through the gift of the Holy Spirit.

We, too, are His disciples. (John 8:31) "And this is how we know that he lives in us; we know it by the Spirit he gave us." (1 John 3:24) That is why our normal should be better than the Old Testament normal. With God living in us, we can know Him more intimately than anyone who could experience Him only in fleeting encounters.

Only by giving us the Holy Spirit could Jesus leave the earth without leaving us as orphans. "Those who are led by the Spirit of God are the children of God. The Spirit you received does not make you slaves, so that you live in fear again; rather, the Spirit you received brought about your adoption to sonship. And by him we cry, '*Abba*, Father.' The Spirit himself testifies with our spirit that we are God's children." (Romans 8:14-16)

We are children of God. The Holy Spirit within us testifies that this is true. And if it is true, it is the truest thing about us and the most wonderful form of acceptance we could possibly ask of God. The Holy Spirit is like a continual hug from our heavenly Father. He holds us in God's constant embrace. We should live on the verge of keeling over from too much love.

If Jesus had stayed on earth, He would have been limited by His physical body. He could have been in only one place at a time, impacting only a limited number of people at once. The Holy Spirit is not limited to one physical body. He inhabits every Christian on earth. "Do you not know that you yourselves are God's temple and that God's Spirit lives in you?" (1 Corinthians 3:16, NET) Since the Holy Spirit lives in us, He can give each one of us His "complete and undivided attention at all times."[1]

---

1   Bevere, *Drawing Near*, p. 153.

SILENT PARTNER?

The Holy Spirit is not a silent partner who ministers to us in mysterious ways we can know little about. The New Testament speaks clearly about His role. Here is a partial list of His activity in the lives of believers:

+ "Very truly I tell you, no one can enter the kingdom of God unless they are born of water and the Spirit." (John 3:5)

+ "The Spirit gives life." (John 6:63)

+ "[The church] was strengthened and encouraged by the Holy Spirit." (Acts 9:31, NIV, 1995)

+ "The love of God has been poured out in our hearts by the Holy Spirit who was given to us." (Romans 5:5, NKJV)

+ "The mind governed by the Spirit is life and peace." (Romans 8:6)

+ "And if anyone does not have the Spirit of Christ, they do not belong to Christ." (Romans 8:9)

+ "The Spirit himself testifies with our spirit that we are God's children." (Romans 8:16)

+ "May the God of hope fill you with all joy and peace as you trust in him, so that you may overflow with hope by the power of the Holy Spirit." (Romans 15:13)

+ "And he has identified us as his own by placing the Holy Spirit in our hearts as the first installment that guarantees everything he has promised us." (2 Corinthians 1:22, NLT)

+ "Does God give you the Holy Spirit and work miracles among you because you obey the law? Of course not! It is because you believe the message you heard about Christ." (Galatians 3:5, NLT)

+ "Since we live by the Spirit, let us keep in step with the Spirit." (Galatians 5:25)

+ "Those who live to please the Spirit will harvest everlasting life from the Spirit." (Galatians 6:8, NLT)

+ "We ... worship by the Spirit of God." (Philippians 3:3, NLT)

+ "And this is how we know that he lives in us: We know it by the Spirit he gave us." (1 John 3:24)

As noted, this is only a partial list, though it is by no means a short one. From this sampling of scriptures, it should be absolutely clear that we have no hope of living a Christian life without the gift of the Holy Spirit. It should also be clear that the Holy Spirit operates in the realm of the supernatural. Our disbelief in this area has placed us squarely in the middle of nowhere and has made the Holy Spirit the most feared and avoided subject in Christendom.

As one author put it, "The idea of asking Him to do something for me—specifically, to pour out the Holy Spirit—injected me with deep apprehension. Both possibilities were equally frightening: that He might answer my prayer and that He might not."[2]

Asking God to do this for us puts us into the dangerous arena of having to trust Him. So we attempt to ride the fence by adopting the ridiculous position that God could so bless us if He chose but just doesn't want to.

He *does* want to. The Holy Spirit was first poured out on the day of Pentecost but was also promised to all future generations. "Peter replied, 'Repent and be baptized, every one of you, in the name of Jesus Christ for the forgiveness of your sins. And you will receive the gift of the Holy Spirit. The promise is for you and your children and to all who are far off—for all whom the Lord our God will call.'" (Acts 2:38-39)

---

2   Zeb Bradford Long and Douglas McMurry, *Collapse of the Brass Heaven* (Grand Rapids, MI: Chosen Books, 1994), p. 16.

GRIEVING THE HOLY SPIRIT

According to the Bible, only wicked people claim God has abandoned us. They use it as an excuse for doing whatever they want. "The sins of the people of Israel and Judah are very, very great. The entire land is full of murder; the city is filled with injustice. They are saying, 'The Lord doesn't see it! The Lord has abandoned the land!'" (Ezekiel 9:9, NLT)

Our unfounded fear of the supernatural has caused us to grieve the Spirit of God by denying or minimizing His role in our lives today. This denial is nothing short of a declaration that we have been abandoned. It also violates the nature of the Spirit of God.

Let me use a simple illustration. Frogs are frogs because they do "frog" things. Frogs croak, swim, hop, and eat bugs. Suppose you came home one day to find a frog sitting at a small dining table on your porch sipping iced tea, smoking a cigar, and eating guacamole while enjoying the soothing sounds of the mariachi band (also frogs) standing around him. Faced with this situation, you would either have to change your concept of reality or change your definition of a frog, because frogs cannot violate their nature.

Neither will God violate His.

The way we understand and define God is the only thing that limits His power to work in us and through us. By defining the Holy Spirit from our own human perspective, we have created Him in *our* own image and made Him too small. We must change our understanding and definition of God so that it is consistent with His nature, not ours. It is time for us to expect God to be God, to act like God, and to do "God" things even when He is operating through us.

*T*HE BREAD OF LIFE AND THE BREATH OF LIFE

The word of God is the bread of life. Jesus said, "Man shall not live on bread alone, but on every word that comes from the mouth of God." (Matthew 4:4) Just as we require physical bread to sustain our bodies, we need spiritual bread to sustain our spirits. Without it, we would starve to death spiritually.

Jesus became the living Word, and we observe the fact that His body was broken for us in the act of breaking the bread of communion. Jesus said, "Unless you eat the flesh of the Son of Man, and drink his blood, you have no life in you." (John 6:53) The Word of God sustains us. He is our spiritual food, the daily bread we need for spiritual survival.

In the act of creation "The Lord God formed the man from the dust of the ground. He breathed the breath of life into the man's nostrils, and the man became a living person." (Genesis 2:7, NLT) Without air, we die even more quickly than we would without bread.

One day God brought Ezekiel, by the Spirit, into the middle of a valley full of dry bones. According to Ezekiel:

> Then he said to me, "Prophesy to the breath; prophesy, son of man, and say to it 'This is what the Sovereign Lord says: Come from the four winds O breath, and breathe into these slain, that they may live.'" So I prophesied as He commanded me, and breath entered them; they came to life and stood up on their feet—a vast army.

> Then he said to me: "Son of man, these bones are the whole house of Israel. They say, 'Our bones are dried up and our hope is gone; we are cut off.' Therefore prophesy and say to them, 'This is what the Sovereign Lord says: O my people, I am going to open your graves and bring

you up from them; I will bring you back to the land of Israel. Then you, my people, will know that I am the Lord, when I open your graves and bring you up from them. *I will put my Spirit in you and you will live*, and I will settle you in your own land.'" (Ezekiel 37:9-14, NIV, 1995, author's emphasis)

The Holy Spirit is the breath Ezekiel prophesied about. In our unbelief, we are prone to say, "Our bones are dried up and our hope is gone; we are cut off." But that is not God's heart for us. We are His people. In His words, "You will live."

Just as God breathed life into the man He first created, Jesus breathed on the disciples and told them to "Receive the Holy Spirit." (John 20:22)

When the Spirit came upon the disciples on the day of Pentecost, the sound was like a mighty wind. (Acts 2:2)

Without the breath of the Holy Spirit, we are like dead men walking, spiritual zombies who talk the talk and go through the motions but bring life to no one. Anyone who says we no longer need the Spirit because we now have the Bible is saying we no longer need air because we now have bread. Clearly, we need both.

An Orphan Spirit

As His children, we should know God better than a child can know his earthly father. But by refusing to receive the fullness of the Holy Spirit, we have become orphans by choice. The thing Jesus promised He would never do to us, we have done to ourselves. We have taken on an abandoned, orphan spirit. As a result, we have developed an orphan-view of life rather than a Father-view.

Orphans are survivors by instinct and by nature. Orphans become selfish, self-reliant, and self-sufficient. They take care of themselves.[3] "We feel secure when we have control—when we are holding fast to the pride of our lives."[4] We have become self-made people who just try to figure out most of our lives on our own.[5] It's the American way.

"This is the enemy's one central purpose—to separate us from the Father."[6] Satan has offered, and we have accepted a counterfeit salvation—one that offers forgiveness and the hope of heaven in place of relationship with God the Father, the maker and sustainer of heaven and earth. We have accepted the middle of nowhere in place of "the presence of a loving and strong Father deeply engaged in our lives, to whom we can turn at any time for the guidance, comfort, and provision we need."[7]

Orphans have trouble with hope. They can't be sure they will be taken care of, so they live in fear. Children who have been adopted by the Father have hope for the future because they feel secure in His care today.

It is not too late for us to repent and change. It's time to wake up and realize we have a Father. We must surrender our self-sufficiency and the control it gives us for knowing God and surrendering to Him.[8] We cannot hold on to God and control at the same time.

---

3   Jimmy Evans, *The Journey of Life*, Gateway Church, May 7, 2006.

4   Michael L. Brown, *How Saved Are We?* (Shippensburg, PA: Destiny Image Publishers, 1990), p. 6.

5   John Eldredge, *Fathered by God* (Nashville, TN: Thomas Nelson, 2009), p. 9.

6   Eldredge, *Fathered by God,* p.57.

7   Eldredge, *Fathered by God,* p. xiii.

8   Long and McMurry, *Collapse of the Brass Heaven,* p.135.

Unholy Fear

Perhaps we are afraid of what God might ask of us if we truly surrender to Him. The issue is Lordship: Who is going to be in control? We may also fear that if we surrender control of our lives to the Holy Spirit, He will cause us to do some of the weird things people do in His name. Where does this weirdness come from, anyway?

Not from God. We need to put our minds at rest in this area. The Holy Spirit does not come to take us over like in the movie *Invasion of the Body Snatchers*. He is a complete gentleman and will never take over our bodies and make us do something we don't want to do. That would violate our free will.

There is a difference between supernatural and weird. The Holy Spirit is there to meet us in power when we step out in faith to do God's will. At times, the supernatural may seem strange or even more than a little uncomfortable. But there is purpose to His presence, and His power is most often released when we step out in compassion to serve other people.

Will the Spirit make us different from the rest of the world? I sincerely hope so, especially more loving and gentle. Of the scores of scriptures that speak of His work in our lives, not one says that it is His purpose or desire to make us weird. The scriptures speak of His peace, power, guidance, and many other wonderful things, but not once of weirdness.

The Holy Spirit comes to help us be more like Jesus. Jesus was different, not weird. He was loving and gentle, but also powerful. He healed people, loved people, and spoke the truth.

First and foremost, the Holy Spirit comes to put us in right relationship with God. He gives us access to God as our loving heavenly Father, with the ability to hear from Him and walk in the fullness of His will and His destiny for our lives. That's how Jesus lived, and it's how He wants us to live.

That which man could never do by "being good," God accomplished through His divine plan. Christ became small, coming to earth to show us what abundant life looks like. Then the Holy Spirit came near, close enough to dwell in our hearts. His indwelling makes us powerful enough to live lives that make a difference.

*T*HE LOVE OF THE FATHER

Luke records a parable we commonly call "The Story of the Prodigal Son." I prefer to call it "The Story of the Loving Father." It has become one of my favorite stories about God.

As you probably recall, the story begins with the younger of a man's two sons asking for his inheritance in advance. This act is the ultimate insult to a father. It's as if the son is saying, "Dad, I wish you were dead. I don't want to be your son. I don't want to have anything to do with you, but I want your money—my share of the inheritance. Give it to me now and I'm gone."

The younger son exhibited the rebellious, self-indulgent spirit of Israel: "God doesn't care and he will do nothing; let's have a party." But before long the money ran out and the son hit bottom, taking a job feeding pigs. Then he "came to himself" and realized that his father's house wasn't so bad after all. Knowing that he no longer deserved to be called a son, he decided to go home and ask to be received and treated like a hired servant.

This is where the story gets good. "So he returned home to his father. And while he was still a long way off, his father saw him coming. Filled with love and compassion, he ran to his son, embraced him, and kissed him." (Luke 15:20, NLT) The Modern Language version says, "When he was still a great way off, his father saw him and felt deeply moved and, running, fell on his neck and kissed him."

The father fell on him and kissed him. On the day of Pentecost, the Holy Spirit fell on the disciples. The word for "fell on" in Acts 2 is the same word used in the parable of the prodigal son. His desire is to "capture us in the embrace of heaven, to catch us up in the fullness of God's love."[9]

God is waiting to fall on us the same way He did in the parable and on Pentecost. He offers us so much more than a few encounters with Him over the span of our lives. He offers us intimacy with Him through the gift of the Holy Spirit.

Adoption as Sons and Daughters

Jesus promised not to leave us as orphans. Instead, He gave us the Holy Spirit, the Spirit of adoption. (Romans 8:15) His presence within us declares that we are sons and daughters of God Most High.

The Holy Spirit is the most wonderful and tender gift God gives. He is the gift of intimacy with the Father. God welcomes us unashamedly and without reservation.

Jesus knew the Father better than any man has ever known Him. The way He chose to represent Him is as the loving father, eager to run to us and embrace us. This is the snapshot Jesus would take out of His wallet to show us if we asked to see a picture of God. It is the polar opposite of the angry God/rejected-sinner picture so many of us still seem to have locked into our minds.

---

9 Hayford, *Living the Spirit Formed Life*, pp 127-128.

Everything the prodigal son had done, including his outright rejection of his father, was forgiven. The father didn't even require a reckoning of all the bad things his son had done. He expressed nothing but joy, acceptance, and love. Then he threw a feast. No expense was too great for celebrating the return of his beloved son.

A picture may be worth a thousand words, but it is not nearly enough to help us see and understand God. So God sent His Son to earth to show us what love in action looks like. Jesus became small for us, taking on human likeness to show us the fullness of God. He showed us what it is like to be guided by the Spirit rather than living by law.

*T*HE HEART OF THE MATTER

Jesus walked in step with the Father. He made it clear that His ministry flowed completely from relationship when He told the disciples that He could do only what He saw the Father doing. (John 5:19)

We are no longer required to live our lives trying to measure up to an impossible standard. We have been set free, not to do whatever we want, but to worship Him—to live for God, from the heart. "The former regulation is set aside because it was weak and useless (for the law made nothing perfect), and a better hope is introduced, by which we draw near to God." (Hebrews 7: 18-19)

We have a better hope, and the core element of that hope is drawing near to God, knowing Him. Yet most of us stumble on, clueless. Jesus' life was all about restoring our relationship with the Father. "No one comes to the Father except through me.... Anyone who has seen me has seen the Father." (John 14:6, 9)

God did not give us the Holy Spirit to help us follow a new set of rules and regulations more perfectly. He gave us the Holy Spirit so that He could be the one who rules and regulates our lives as we walk in His guidance and power. His goal is to enable us to hear God's voice so that He can lead us into His will.

It is difficult for us to grasp, but God does not require that we attain perfection in order to have access to Him. He opened the way into His presence for us by the sacrifice of His son Jesus Christ, the sinless, spotless Lamb of God. Jesus became our perfection because we could never attain it. Jesus cleared the way, but the Holy Spirit provides the means: "For through him [Jesus] we both [Jews and Gentiles] have access to the Father by one Spirit." (Ephesians 2:18)

MATTERS OF THE HEART

God's presence is not to be taken lightly. Godly fear requires that we honor Him, holding Him in reverence and awe: "By those who come near Me I must be regarded as holy; and before all the people I must be glorified." (Leviticus 10:3, NKJV) "Let us be thankful, and so worship God acceptably with reverence and awe, for 'our God is a consuming fire.'" (Hebrews 12:29) The Bible is very clear about this: Reverence and awe for God produce an attitude of thanksgiving and worship. This is not worship as in "going to church." It is a lifestyle of submission to His will and bringing glory to His name by the way we live.

A hungry heart comes to God humbly, free of hidden agendas or any hint of manipulation. Humility understands its neediness and seeks God for nothing other than the joy of His presence: "My flesh and my heart may fail, but God is the strength of my heart and my portion forever." (Psalm 73:26) "Listen, listen to me, and eat what is good, and you will delight in the richest of fare.... Seek the Lord while he may be found; call on him while he is near." (Isaiah 55:2, 6)

The Lord is near those who seek Him today:

✴ "'You will seek me and find me when you seek me with all your heart. I will be found by you,' declares the Lord." (Jeremiah 29:13-14)

✴ "The Lord is near to all who call on him, to all who call on him in truth." (Psalm 145:18)

✴ "Come near to God, and he will come near to you." (James 4:8)

If there is any distance between God and us today, He is not the one who put it there. He eagerly waits for us to turn to Him. He is anxious to run to meet us, to fall on us, and to give us all the riches of His house.

Relationship takes an investment of our time and energy, an investment of ourselves. You would never reveal your deepest thoughts and secrets to someone who doesn't care about you or take the time to be with you. You won't make yourself known to someone who always seems bored, distracted, or in a hurry to leave when you are around. Neither will God.

To those willing to make the investment, God wants to make Himself known. Just as a radio is equipped to pick up radio waves, we are equipped to hear His voice. A radio picks up radio waves because someone has placed a receiver inside it. God has given us something way better. The Holy Spirit allows us to hear from the eternal God who placed Him within us. Deep calls to deep (Psalm 42:7), allowing us to walk in step with our supernatural creator.

God has spoken to us in many ways in the past, and there is no scriptural evidence that He has put aside any of these tools. We should be open to God speaking to us in any of these biblical ways:

+ Through circumstances (Jonah 1:4)
+ Through nature (Psalm 18:13, Psalm 19:1-3)
+ Through the wise counsel of other people (Esther 4:12-14)
+ Through a prophetic word (Acts 21:10-11)
+ Through the Bible (2 Timothy 3:16)
+ Through peace (Colossians 3:15)
+ Through thoughts (Amos 4:13)
+ Through supernatural manifestations (2 Kings 20:11, Daniel 5:5)
+ Through an animal (Numbers 22:28)
+ Through dreams and visions (Numbers 12:6, Acts 2:17)
+ Through a whisper (1 Kings 19:12)
+ In an audible voice (1 Samuel 3:4)
+ Through angels (Judges 6:12, Luke 2:9)
+ Under the power of the Spirit (Ezekiel 37:1, Revelation 4:2)
+ Face to face (Numbers12:7-8)
+ In our hearts (Ephesians 1:18, Acts 16:14)

As I think about some of the stories in which God spoke to men—the story of Jonah, for example—I realize that these are some of the most wonderful and unusual stories in the Bible. Our rational, reasonable, modern minds have trouble believing these stories actually occurred. How could a fish be sent to swallow a man? How could Jonah have survived for three days in the hostile environment of the fish's stomach? Is the Bible myth or truth?

These stories cut to the essence of our faith. To disbelieve closes the door to the supernatural. It relegates God to being detached and far away, a God who tells a great story and who will do something someday, but not for us, not today. To believe opens the door to a wonderful, almost unimaginable world of possibility in which God is near and still at work. It sets us up for ridicule from our peers, but it also calls us to a life in which it is actually possible to hear from God and to be used by Him.

*A*CTING LIKE *S*ONS

When I do something the way my father would do it, I demonstrate that I know my father. I was born into his household. I lived in relationship with him for many years. I saw him do many things and heard him explain why certain things should be done in certain ways. When I act like my father, I show myself to be his son.

Sons do things out of relationship, not out of obligation or fear. If we acted like God's sons we would act more like Jesus. Jesus made a difference. His life counted. It had impact.

Jesus had a destiny and He fulfilled it. He knew the Father and always did what the Father would do. (John 5:19). A lot of those things were miraculous.

If we want to know how to please God, we must learn to be better sons and daughters.

* ✚ *

CHAPTER 6

THE SPIRIT OF WISDOM *and* REVELATION

How much more will your Father in heaven give the
Holy Spirit to those who ask him?

LUKE 11:13

VICTORY

When what was left of the Midianite army fled, Gideon sent for the men of Ephraim to cut off their escape route at the fords of the Jordan River. There they captured Oreb and Zeeb, two of the Midianite leaders. They beheaded them and presented their heads to Gideon when he arrived at the Jordan.

Gideon and his exahusted 300 men went beyond the Jordan in pursuit of the Midianite kings, Zebah and Zalmunna. After they were captured, Gideon killed them both with his sword. Victory was finally complete.

I can picture Gideon lifting his hands in praise to God while the men raised a great shout of victory. This was the moment for which he had been born. The Midianites were defeated. Leaderless, they would not be quick to return.

God had given Gideon a warrior spirit because that's what was needed in his time. He became a mighty warrior because God knew that's what it would take to deliver Israel. Gideon was purpose-built and God-supplied.

*G*OOD GIFTS

So are we. God has designed each of us with particular strengths and giftings. Our acceptable worship to Him consists of using our abilities to accomplish His purposes and bring Him glory.

God always gives good gifts. He gave us Christ for Christmas. His purpose was to provide us with salvation, life, and hope. Jesus made it clear that after His ascension, He would not leave us as orphans. On the day of Pentecost, God poured out the gift of the Holy Spirit—the Spirit of adoption—on His children. This gift was so important that the disciples were told not to do anything or go anywhere before receiving it. (Acts 1:4-5)

I KEEP ASKING

The apostle Paul recognized the importance of this gift, not only for himself, but for all Christians. He had one thing that he kept asking God. There was one blessing he knew the church could never succeed without. "I keep asking that the God of our Lord Jesus Christ, the glorious Father, may give you the Spirit of wisdom and revelation, so that you may know him better." (Ephesians 1:17)

Think about the apostle Paul. After his conversion he devoted his entire life to the church. For its sake he endured beatings, shipwrecks, imprisonment, stoning, and finally martyrdom at the hands of the Romans. Do you think he carefully considered the things the church needed? Do you think he was deliberate in choosing how to pray for it? Of course he was. He knew where Satan would attack the church, and he diligently defended it in prayer. His words, like the words of Gideon's messenger, were carefully chosen.

Paul asked that the Father give the gift of the Holy Spirit—whom Christ promised in John 14:16—to the church at Ephesus. This gift was meant to impart spiritual wisdom and revelation to the Christians there for one purpose: knowing the Father. "Now this is eternal life: that they know you, the only true God, and Jesus Christ, whom you have sent." (John 17:3)

Knowing God

If you asked Christians today what Christianity is, how many would say that first and foremost it consists of knowing God? They might say Christianity is about going to church regularly, studying the Word, praying, or living good lives.

But these things are peripheral. At its very heart, Christianity is having relationship with God. For this we need the Spirit of wisdom and revelation.

God's desire is that we know Him. "Knowing God is the primary purpose of Man—to know Him intimately; to know His heart; to know how He thinks; to know His personal interest in us; to know … how He relates."[1]

With the indwelling of the Spirit, we have communion with God, our source. Spirit-supplied wisdom connects us with

1 Hayford, *Grounds for Living,* p.29.

God and gives us the ability to hear His voice. He gives us spiritual ears to hear spiritual things.

Wisdom teaches us to hear God's perspective. It gives comprehensive insight into the ways and purposes of God.

In like manner, the Spirit of revelation enables us to see the things of God. When Elijah asked God to open the eyes of his servant, he saw the surrounding hills filled with horses and chariots of fire. (2 Kings 6:17) They had been there all along, but it took opened eyes — the eyes of revelation — to see them.

There is a spiritual world far more real, lasting, and important than the world we now inhabit. But since we are accustomed to our concrete surroundings, we tend to think of reality in terms of our environment. We tend to see ourselves as physical bodies inhabited by a spiritual person rather than as spiritual people who are temporarily housed in a physical body.

But the spiritual world is everything. "Who you are at the core is spirit. God is Spirit. To walk with God is to journey in the spiritual realm."[2] When we view reality from the physical perspective, we can easily lose track of the things that are really important. We can develop spiritual blindness and deafness.

These issues were central to the way people received Jesus' ministry. Jesus told the disciples, "For this people's heart has become calloused; they hardly hear with their ears, and they have closed their eyes. Otherwise, they might see with their eyes, hear with their ears, understand with their hearts and turn, and I would heal them. But blessed are your eyes, because they see, and your ears, because they hear." (Mat-

---

2 McManus, *The Barbarian Way*, p. 61.

thew 13:15-16) The condition of our eyes and ears makes all
the difference.

For most of us, our eyes and ears are the primary means
by which we take information into our brains for processing.
They alert us to physical danger, help us find food and
water, and help us accomplish tasks. Spiritual eyes and ears
take information into the heart for processing. When they
function as God intended, they alert us to spiritual danger,
help us understand the Bible or biblical teaching, and help us
accomplish the work God has in mind for us to do.

Wisdom versus Knowledge

The dwelling place of wisdom is in the heart (Proverbs 2:10,
Proverbs 14:33). The dwelling place of knowledge is in the
head. While the Bible can give us head-knowledge of God, it
is only through the Holy Spirit that we can really know God
deeply and intimately, from the heart.

We see this distinction clearly in Jesus' comments concerning the Pharisees. Jesus told them, "You have your heads
in your Bibles constantly because you think you'll find eternal
life there." (John 5:39, *The Message*) The Pharisees' reliance
on their head-knowledge of the scriptures actually caused
them to reject Jesus. He condemned them with these startling
words: "You have never heard his [the Father's] voice, nor
seen his form, nor does his word dwell in you." (John 5:38)

In spite of all the time they spent in the scriptures, the Word
did not dwell in them, and they had never heard the Father's
voice. Their emphasis on head-knowledge of the scriptures
only served to harden their hearts, so that when Jesus called

them they were unable to hear His voice. Head-knowledge of God is not enough to save us.

The Pharisees were victims of their own wisdom. But it doesn't have to be that way for us:

> What we have received is not the spirit of the world, but the Spirit who is from God, so that we may understand what God has freely given us. This is what we speak, not in words taught us by human wisdom but in words taught by the Spirit, explaining spiritual realities with Spirit-taught words. The person without the Spirit does not accept the things that come from the Spirit of God but considers them foolishness, and cannot understand them, because they are discerned only through the Spirit.
> (1 Corinthians 2:12-14)

Only the Holy Spirit can give us true wisdom. He alone can teach us the ways of God. "The particular foolishness of the church in the past century was Reason above all else. The result has been a faith stripped of the supernatural, the Christianity of tips and techniques."[3]

True wisdom gives us the ability to hear God's voice. Anytime we hear God's voice, our faith will grow: "So then, faith comes by hearing, and hearing by the word of God." (Romans 10:17, NKJV)

When Gideon heard God's voice, his faith began to grow, and it finally grew to the point where he was ready to fight the Midianites, even with only 300 men. When God spoke to Moses from the burning bush, Moses' level of faith was raised to the point where he was willing to confront Pharaoh.

If God has stopped speaking, or if we have stopped listening, our faith has stopped growing. This produces one of

---

3   Eldredge, *Waking the Dead,* p. 101.

two results: either we will have the faith to do nothing, or we will have faith enough to do only what we can do in our own strength.

Fortunately, Solomon was not the only human to whom God made wisdom available. James tells us, "If any of you lacks wisdom, you should ask God, who gives generously to all without finding fault, and it will be given to you." (James 1:5) God is not a respecter of persons, nor does He desire to withhold from us the things we need. He wants to speak to us, and He has given us His Spirit to help us hear Him. We can know Him, not just know *about* Him.

THE SPIRIT OF WISDOM

Wisdom is the first of God's works:

> I [wisdom] walk in the way of righteousness, along the paths of justice, bestowing a rich inheritance on those who love me and making their treasuries full.
>
> The Lord brought me forth as the first of his works, before his deeds of old; I was formed long ages ago, at the very beginning, when the world came to be....
>
> I was there when he set the heavens in place, when he marked out the horizon on the face of the deep....
>
> Then I was constantly at his side, I was filled with delight day after day, rejoicing always in his presence, rejoicing in his whole world and delighting in mankind." (Proverbs 8:20-31)

By turning away from the gift of the Holy Spirit, we have forsaken wisdom and lost track of its great value. Wisdom was established by God—not created. Birthed from His very nature, wisdom stood by God as His craftsman in the epic days of creation. Wisdom and God are inseparable. Finding wisdom brings life and favor. The Spirit of God longs to help us find all of wisdom's benefits. We forsake the Spirit of wisdom to our own detriment and to the detriment of those whose lives we impact.

Listen once more to wisdom's voice: "I was filled with delight day after day, rejoicing always in his presence, rejoicing in his whole world and delighting in mankind." This same voice could be ours. It describes a way we could live every day. It is the way of wisdom.

*W*ISDOM FOR THE WAY

When Solomon asked the Lord for wisdom in 2 Chronicles 1:10, he literally asked for a listening heart. True spiritual wisdom is the ability to hear God in our hearts, where He most often speaks to us. We must have spiritual ears attuned to hear.

Remember when the Israelites chose the wrong kind of fear on Mount Sinai? Their fear separated them from God. As a result, they were unwilling and unable to hear God's voice and to receive His wisdom.

They had it backward. The inability to hear God's voice is the very thing that placed them on the path of death. Because they could not hear Him, they missed the opportunity to enter the Promised Land. As a result, they wandered in the wilderness and died.

Moses, on the other hand, chose to approach God in holy fear. What is holy fear? Awe is probably the best word for it. It is the awe of God that causes us to want to press into His presence and worship Him.

As a result, the Bible tells us that Moses knew God's ways, while Israel knew only His acts. (Psalm 103:7) In other words, Israel could see what God did only from an external perspective. They had to have laws to guide them because they were clueless about God's ways. Moses came to know God's heart through an ongoing relationship. Only by knowing God could he know God's ways.

THE SPIRIT OF REVELATION

According to tradition, Christopher Columbus used to sit on the dock and watch ships sail out to sea. Supposedly, he noticed that the ships sailing away from the harbor disappeared gradually from bottom to top. From this observation, he figured out that the earth was round and that the ships disappeared in this fashion because of the curvature of the earth. Based on this understanding, he decided that he could sail west to reach the east. His discovery of America was a serendipitous result of his attempt to find a new trading route to the Far East.

If tradition is accurate, Columbus saw something anyone else could have seen, but didn't. There are two ways to be found sittin' on the dock of the bay. One way is the non-seeing, time-wasting way Otis Redding sang about. The other is with eyes that see differently, eyes that have been opened to see something new. These are eyes that are open to revelation.

Revelation is:

+ The act of revealing or communicating truth
+ Making something known by bringing it into view
+ Showing, unveiling, or making something manifest

The picture that comes to mind is that of an artist unveiling a new sculpture. To that point the unfinished piece has been locked away, out of sight, until the work is completed. Then it is moved to its final resting place, still hidden by a tarp or other covering. At the proper moment, the covering is pulled away and the work is revealed for the world to see, to the requisite ooohs and aaaahs of the crowd. Another way to say it is that the artwork has been brought into the light. That which was hidden is now visible.

Spiritual revelation, then, is when God brings into the light something that has been hidden. Perhaps the most obvious example is the book of Revelation in the Bible. God gave John a series of visions to reveal things that were to come. God can, and often does, use dreams and visions to bring us revelation. (Job 33:15) But He doesn't have to. Something He shows us in our heart can also be revelation.

Revelation is about having spiritual eyes that see spiritual things. According to the Bible, these spiritual eyes reside in our heart. God wants to give us eyes to see, but what would God want to reveal to us? He has already given us all the Scripture we need. (2 Timothy 3:16, 17)

Among other things, God wants to show us how to have our hearts healed. And He wants us to know whom we were created to be.

The most important thing we could ever see is God's father-heart toward us. We need to see Him in a new way—the way He really is.

*R*ULES VERSUS REVELATION

A certain pastor had two alcoholic friends. One day the Lord put it on his heart to buy one of them a gold watch. On the back of the watch, he had a specific scripture inscribed. When he gave it to his friend, it changed his life. He gave up alcohol and began to serve God.

Buoyed by this success, the pastor quickly bought another gold watch. He then had a scripture inscribed on the back of it and gave it to his other alcoholic friend. That man sold the watch and used the proceeds to buy more alcohol.[4]

This story is rich with lessons. What the man did for his first friend came through revelation. Somehow, he had heard from God. As soon as he did, he knew what to do: Buy the friend a watch and put an inscription on it. And because God told him to do it, it worked.

God knows everything, so He can tell us what will work. He is the author of effective strategy, and He can reveal such strategies to us if we will listen.

But the same strategy didn't work for the second friend. Why? Because it wasn't through revelation. The pastor tried to take revelation from God and make it into a rule: "Every alcoholic friend will be transformed by the gift of a gold watch with a scripture inscribed on the back."

We almost always want to make revelation into law. Following law is so much easier than walking in revelation. Westerners struggle with a Christianity that is based on relationship rather than rules. Rules are rational and safe. They deal with actions rather than with the heart. They can be rationalized away or just plain ignored.

Revelation is superior to law. But revelation is hard. Revelation requires seeking and then demands action. It calls for obedience, even when obedience is risky or inconvenient. It

4   Bruce Larson, *Setting Men Free* (Grand Rapids, MI, Zondervan Publishing House, 1972), pp. 86, 87.

takes sacrifice and commitment to hammer out a relation-ship with God that works on the principles of hear, believe, and obey.

We like rules because we are problem oriented. We want problems solved, and we think problems can be solved with equations such as this one: Hear + Believe + Repent + Confess = Eternal Life. But Jesus gave this formula: "Now this is eternal life: that they may know you, the only true God, and Jesus Christ, whom you have sent." (John 17:3) Know God + Know Jesus = Eternal Life.

Revelation works on a level entirely different from rules or law—the level of the heart. Rules are for solving problems. Revelation is for solving lives.[5]

Jesus lived by revelation. He did only what He saw God doing. That is why He never healed two blind men the same way. It's why He was always in the right spot at the right time saying or doing the right thing. And the same Spirit of revelation available to Him is also available to us.

God is a self-revealing God. He desires to reveal himself to us. Our pastors can teach us about God, but they cannot know God for us. God gives us the Spirit of wisdom and revelation so that we may hear Him and walk in obedience to Him. We must press into God in a lifestyle of worship to experience the fullness of life He offers.

Let our testimony be that we are not of those who shrink back and live in defeat, but of those who believe, press in, and experience the fullness of salvation, both now and forever.

What We Have Seen and Heard

Every part of spiritual life starts with seeing or hearing. The

---

5   Eldredge, *Waking the Dead*, p. 93

wise men sought Jesus after they saw His star in the east. (Matthew 2:2) Jesus saw the crowds, had compassion on them, and healed them. (Matthew 14:14) The disciples saw that the fig tree had withered. (Matthew 21:20) The people heard John the Baptist as the voice of one crying in the wilderness. (Matthew 3:3) Jesus spoke to the people in parables. (Matthew 13:13) The Pharisees heard Jesus' answer to their question and were amazed. (Matthew 22:22)

The disciples came to understand this concept. When they were persecuted for teaching about Jesus, they told their persecutors, "As for us, we cannot help speaking about what we have seen and heard." (Acts 4:20)

We live in a time when very few Christians are vocal about their faith. They go to work or school, go home, watch television, and go to church. But for the most part, nothing about their lives seems to be worth sharing. There is a notable lack of passion concerning their Christianity.

As much as it pains me, I have to ask one question: Could it be that most Christians haven't seen or heard anything?

Witnesses

Suppose you witnessed a terrible traffic accident on your way to work. What is the first thing you would talk about when you got to your workplace? Or suppose you heard an amazing new song—the best song ever—by your favorite group. Wouldn't you be eager to tell someone who shared your passion?

What if God gave you a word for someone that you knew would change their life? What if you saw someone healed from a lifelong disease? What if the presence of the Holy Spirit became palpable in your church? Wouldn't you want to tell somebody?

Imagine that one day you went to court to testify in a murder case. You took the stand and the lawyer began to ask you questions.

"Did you see someone murder John Doe on the night of August 2nd in downtown Fort Worth?"

"No."

"Did you hear anything that would shed light on the case?"

"No."

"Where were you on the night of August 2?"

"I was in Little Rock."

"Then why are you here?"

"I just wanted to testify."

After you were thrown out of the courtroom, or possibly into jail, everyone would talk about your ridiculous behavior. You cannot testify unless you are a witness, and you are not a witness unless you have seen or heard something.

Jesus told His followers, "But you will receive power when the Holy Spirit comes on you; and you will be my witnesses in Jerusalem, and in all Judea and Samaria, and to the ends of the earth." (Acts 1:8) The power of the Holy Spirit and the ability to be witnesses are connected. By His power we see and hear. Then we cannot help but testify.

God understands our nature because He created us. We were made to share the things that are important to us—things that are significant, meaningful, or beautiful—things we have seen and heard. We serve a God who is the most significant, meaningful, and beautiful being in existence. And we live among people who are desperate for Him—and for the life He offers. But we cannot share what we do not have.

Having seen and heard gives us hope for lives that make a difference. Let's examine how Peter came to this revelation.

* ✦ *

CHAPTER 7

I'M GOING FISHING

I pray that the eyes of your heart may be enlightened
in order that you may know the hope
to which he has called you....

EPHESIANS 1:18

THE FISHERMAN'S SON

Peter thought he knew who he was. He was the son of a fisherman, and in Peter's day the son became his father's apprentice, learned how to do his father's work, and took over his father's business. Peter and his brother Andrew were fishermen, and that was what they always would be.

Then one day a man named Jesus walked up to Peter and asked if He could use his boat. Not for fishing, but for preaching. The crowds were large and Jesus needed space. He asked Peter to row out a short distance into the water so the people could not press in upon Him—a watery form of crowd control.

With Jesus in his boat, Peter was a captive audience. He was also captivated by the things Jesus had to say. He had never heard anything like it. But Jesus' sermon was not the thing of importance that day. The Bible doesn't even record it. The important thing was what Jesus did next.

Once Jesus finished His message to the people, He had a message for Peter. He asked him to row farther out to sea and let down his net. Simon was probably a little irritated by this. You can almost hear it in his response to Jesus, "Master, we've worked hard all night and haven't caught anything. But because you say so, I will let down the nets." (Luke 5:5) Interpretation: "Why don't you stick to preaching and let me do the fishing? We haven't caught anything and we ain't gonna. It's the wrong time of day for this foolishness."

*W*HAT PETER SAW AND HEARD

You know the rest of the story. Peter caught so many fish they were breaking his net. Peter saw something—a miraculous catch of fish. Clearly this Jesus was someone special.

But old mindsets are hard to break. Peter was impressed with Jesus but could not imagine Jesus being impressed with him. He could not see himself as part of the story. His humble response was, "Go away from me Lord; I am a sinful man!" (Luke 5:8) It was a Gideon-like response. "Please move on and find a better man—someone worthy, somebody with more potential."

Peter's response was basically that of the cartoon character, Popeye: "I yam what I yam. I yam a sinful fisherman, Lord, and I yam not likely to ever be anything more." These words anticipate neither growth nor change. They are "the sad cry of the human race. You have said these words in your own way, and so have I."[1] They are the words of hope deferred.

---

1   John Ortberg, *The Life You've Always Wanted,* p. 14.

But Jesus did not see Peter the fisherman. He saw Peter on down the line, after being transformed by the power of the Holy Spirit. Jesus spoke from what *He* saw, not what Peter could see. His words changed Peter's life. "Don't be afraid. From now on you will fish for people." (Luke 5:10) Peter heard something—a call from the Lord to a whole new identity.

Even so, three years later Peter was ready to go back to his old vocation. Jesus had been crucified and, three days later, had risen from the dead. Peter had seen Jesus on two occasions since His resurrection but still remained lost and confused. He had disappointed Jesus, and Jesus had disappointed him by not setting up His kingdom on earth. He was uncomfortable in the Master's presence. He felt sure he would be rejected for having denied Jesus. So, Peter did what was logical to him. He fell back on something safe and secure. He told the other disciples, "I'm going fishing." (John 21:3, *The Message*)

Identity

The struggle for your identity is intense. Why? Because the enemy fears you. "If you find out who you are, you will rise up and be a great threat to his work. You'll live extraordinarily and bring great pleasure to your heavenly Father."[2]

Like Peter, we will always fail Jesus at some point. Satan will then use our sense of disappointment to try to sidetrack us from our destiny. He will try to tell us that we are what we are and no more. But Jesus doesn't dwell on our failures. He is not put off by our lives in the present tense. He sees our potential.

Fortunately for Peter and the rest of us, Jesus had more to say to Peter. Jesus met the disciples at the lake and called to

---

2   John Bevere, *Extraordinary* (Colorado Springs, CO: Waterbrook Press, 2009), p. 143.

them from the shore. He told them to cast the net on the right side of the boat. They did, and it was *déjà vu* all over again. The net was filled with 153 large fish, but this time it did not break. (John 21:5-11)

After pulling the net to shore, Peter still was at a loss for words. He dared neither to ask Jesus to leave nor beg him to stay. So Jesus cut straight to the issue. He asked Peter if he loved Him. He asked him three times, once for each of Peter's denials. Then He put His stamp on Peter's future by telling him, "Feed my lambs." (John 21:16) Interpretation: "I have not rejected you. I still have a plan for you, and I am still the key to your destiny. You are not a fisherman. You will establish my church and take care of my people."

*H*OPE AND PURPOSE

Satan wants to keep God's will from being done on earth. One way he does this is by attacking God's purpose in life for each one of God's children. If he can attack our destinies, he can keep us from accomplishing the things God has purposed for us.

Satan would like to convince us that the present does not matter that much to God, and even if it does we are too weak or too flawed or too sinful for the task at hand. He shames us to the point we are ready to give up. We dare not talk to Jesus, especially to ask Him to be near. Our only hope seems to be to fall back on whatever is comfortable to us until one fine day when Jesus will return and set up His kingdom.

Our defense against this attack is enlightenment of the heart. Only the Holy Spirit can open us to the hope to which we have been called. It takes the gift of enlightenment to see that God is bigger than our fallback position. He is bigger than the fish, the net, the boat, and the lake.

It is impossible for us to have hope for today without understanding that God is invested in our lives; He cares about us in the present. When we come to understand this present hope, the doorway to our destiny opens.

God still speaks. "He makes the power of His Spirit, the power of His word, and the nearness of His presence available to you. All those things contain the very force that spoke the world into existence and they have the power to restore you to the life for which you were intended."[3]

Failure: Success that does not Matter to God

Picture yourself at a train station trying to pick between two trains pointed in opposite directions. The trains look similar, and each train is named "Success," but underneath each name is a subtitle that is small and hard to read. When you try to concentrate on the subtitles, someone seems in a hurry to distract you and tell you that his train is the one you want to be on. That someone is Satan.

In fact, the subtitles are very, very important. One train is called "Success: Getting ahead in the world the best way I know how." The other is called "Success: Submitting to God's plan for moving me to my destiny." Satan makes his train look as much like God's as possible, but the real name of his train is "Failure: Success that does not matter to God."[4] Needless to say, if Satan can get us on the wrong train, he is perfectly happy to let us run in the right direction once the train starts moving.

---

3   Bob Hamp, *Think Differently, Live Differently*, p. 210.

4   Graham Cooke, *Developing Your Prophetic Gifting* (Tonbridge, Kent, England: Sovereign World Ltd., 1994) p. 255.

No matter our intentions, we have believed God will do little or nothing to impact our present lives. We have made Him small. We have pictured Him to be distant. We have relegated Him to the future and the past. We have painted God into the corner of irrelevancy and behaved as if we live under an inferior covenant. We have acted as if His Spirit does not live within us. Out of touch with our Father, our lives are guided by circumstance. No wonder we have lost hope.

Biblical hope is neither wishing for the things we want nor resigning ourselves to life without them. It is an unshakable expectation that God will do what He has said He will do. It comes from enlightenment of the heart and is based on the character and the purposefulness of God. "For I know the plans I have for you," declares the Lord, "plans to prosper you and not to harm you, plans to give you hope and a future." (Jeremiah 29:11) Notice that God's plans are to give us hope *and* a future, not just hope *for* the future. If we believed God rather than just believing *in* God, we would say with the psalmist, "My hope is in you all day long." (Psalm 25:5)

Seven Pillars of Hope

Biblical hope is based on God, not on our own human effort or worthiness. It rests on seven unshakable, eternal pillars.[5]

+ *Knowing God.* He is the King of Kings and the Lord of Lords. He is the creator and sustainer of the universe. He is the Alpha and the Omega, the Eternal God. He is God Almighty, the Lord of Angel Armies. He is the one true, all-powerful, all-encompassing, all-knowing God. He is the King of Glory. He is high and lifted up, exalted above the heavens and the earth. There is none beside Him.

---

5   Cooke, *Developing Your Prophetic Gifting*, pp. 257-258.

+ *Knowing His character.* He is love and He is truth. He is perfection and light. He cannot lie. The angels who surround Him cannot refrain from crying, "Holy, holy, holy is the Lord God Almighty, who was, and is, and is to come." (Revelation 4:8)

+ *Knowing His nature.* He is God. He is faithful, merciful, gracious, kind, and forgiving. He always keeps His promises. He is supernatural and He does supernatural things. He always has and He always will.

+ *Knowing His heart toward us.* "He is the kindest Person I have ever known. He is my Father, he has chosen me and set his love upon me."[6] He has loved me with an everlasting love. He has plans to prosper me and not to harm me. He has never had one unkind thought toward me. He wants to have fellowship with me.

+ *Knowing where He has placed me.* God has put me in Christ, the one place where I can always find favor and acceptance—the one place where he will hear my prayers and I will hear his voice."[7] In Christ, "neither death nor life, neither angels nor demons, neither the present nor the future, nor any powers, neither height nor depth, nor anything else in all creation will be able to separate [me] from the love of God that is in Christ Jesus our Lord." (Romans 8:38-39)

+ *Knowing His power.* He spoke the universe into existence. He knows every star by name. He parted the Red Sea, protected Daniel in the lion's den, surrounded Elijah with chariots of fire, raised Jesus from the dead, poured out the Holy Spirit on Pentecost, and promised that the very same Holy Spirit would dwell within us and work through us.

+ *Knowing He cannot change.* "Jesus Christ is the same yesterday and today and forever." (Hebrews 13:8) "I the Lord do not change." (Malachi 3:6) God has not gone

---

6 Cooke, *Developing Your Prophetic Gifting*, p. 257.

7 Cooke, *Developing Your Prophetic Gifting,* p. 258.

out of business, and He has not changed the way He does business. For us to expect Him not to act like God in our generation is foolish and unbelieving. We can change our unbiblical understanding and definition of God. We can expect God to be consistent with His nature, not ours.

Making God Small

You may well be asking yourself, "Are these things really possible in this day and age, or is this guy insane?" I propose that the real insanity of our time is continuing in the same old lifeless behaviors that have gone on for generations and expecting different results. It was not working for Gideon, and it is not working for us. If what the church in America has been doing was going to change anything, it would have done so by now.

"We have lost the glory, the majesty, and the mystery of all that God is within himself...the mystery and the majesty of God are not optional extras but the very proof of our life in him."[8] In losing God's majesty, we have lost the art of worship.

Because we have made our God too small, we have settled for small lives and small victories. This has resulted in the church having too small an impact on our culture. It is time for us to realize that God is our hope.

Biblical hope expects God to be God, to act like God, and to do God things. Hope takes a stand; it takes sides with God. Hope gives us a reason to seek God's face. Hope leads to expectation that God might actually do something—now. It puts joy in our hearts and purpose in our steps; it gives

---

8   Graham Cooke, *A Divine Confrontation* (Shippensburg, PA: Destiny Image Publishers, 1999), p. 20.

meaning to prayer and puts positive confession on our lips. "I believed, therefore I have spoken." (2 Corinthians 4:13)

The Bible says, "The Lord delights in those who fear him, who put their hope in his unfailing love." (Psalm 147:11) We have an opportunity to delight God. If we would walk in hope, we could begin to understand His plans for us. We could find our identity and the purpose for which we were created.

God's purpose for Israel after the exodus was to bring His chosen people to Himself. But at Mount Sinai they drew back from His presence. They chose ungodly fear instead of the fear of the Lord. They chose to be afraid of God instead of worshipping Him.

Worship is not "going to church," and it is more than singing songs. Worship is giving God "the place of glory, honor, reverence, thanksgiving, praise, and preeminence He deserves"[9] in our lives.

Israel did not want to give God that much control. They wanted, not the freedom to worship, but the freedom to do whatever they wanted. Because they drew back from God, they could not come to know Him. Without knowing God they knew neither wisdom nor hope. This caused them to draw back from their destiny. As a result, God's purpose for Israel was delayed for an entire generation. Of that generation God would later say, "Their hearts are always going astray, and they have not known my ways." (Hebrews 3:10)

Today if You Will Hear His Voice

In Hebrews there is a lengthy but powerful passage that offers us a much better alternative than hopeless and empty lives.

---

9 Bevere, *Extraordinary,* p.30.

You have not come to a mountain that can be touched and that is burning with fire; to darkness, gloom, and storm; to a trumpet blast or to such a voice speaking words that those who heard it begged that no further words be spoken to them, because they could not bear what was commanded: "If even an animal touches the mountain, it must be stoned to death." The sight was so terrifying that Moses said, "I am trembling with fear."

But you have come to Mount Zion, to the city of the living God, the heavenly Jerusalem. You have come to thousands upon thousands of angels in joyful assembly, to the church of the firstborn, whose names are written in heaven. You have come to God, the Judge of all, to the spirits of the righteous made perfect, to Jesus the mediator of a new covenant, and to the sprinkled blood that speaks a better word than the blood of Abel.

See to it that you do not refuse him who speaks. If they did not escape when they refused him who warned them on earth, how much less will we, if we turn away from him who warns us from heaven? At that time his voice shook the earth, but now he has promised, "Once more I will shake not only the earth but also the heavens." The words "once more" indicate the removing of what can be shaken—that is, created things—so that what cannot be shaken may remain.

Therefore, since we are receiving a kingdom that cannot be shaken, let us be thankful, and so worship God accept-ably with reverence and awe, for our God is a consuming fire. (Hebrews 12:18-29)

Do not refuse Him who speaks. It is all about God. It always has been, and it always will be. He invites us to draw near. "'But my righteous one will live by faith. And I take no pleasure in the one who shrinks back.' But we do not belong to those who shrink back and are destroyed, but to those who have faith and are saved." (Hebrews 10:38-39) Our calling is to worship Him acceptably and to hear His voice. "See to it, brothers and sisters, that none of you has a sinful, unbelieving heart that turns away from the living God.... 'Today, if you hear his voice, do not harden your hearts, as you did in the rebellion.'" (Hebrews 3:12, 15)

God is fully invested in today. He still speaks and we can hear Him. But we have stopped listening because we have convinced ourselves that God has nothing else to say. We have hardened our hearts. In our own way we have said to each other, "I don't know what else to do. I'm going fishing." This attitude can never produce transformation.

Instead, we are invited to lovingly submit to Jesus. "And he who loves Me will be loved by my Father, and I too will love him and manifest Myself to him." (John 14:21b, NKJV)

Jesus always keeps His promises, and He has promised to manifest Himself to us. To make something manifest means to bring it into the light. Jesus wants to reveal Himself to us, to enlighten us about His identity and character. When we see Him we can experience true transformation.

Jesus is our only hope for change that really matters. This hope is based on the nature and character of Jesus, not on our performance. (Hebrews 10:19-23)

We tend to settle for inferior hope because we cannot convince ourselves that God's heart toward us is good. Like Simon Peter, we cannot believe God can see anything good in us, so we cannot see ourselves as part of the picture. But the evidence to the contrary is overwhelming: 1) the price He paid for us, 2) the promises He has made to us, 3) the unchanging nature of God, 4) His incredible grace and mercy, 5) His character (He is love).

When we understand His heart, it changes our entire attitude toward Him. He is our loving Father, our friend and ally, the only one who is powerful enough to change us. We see that He created us for a purpose, and we can move in faith toward our destinies.

*T*HUNDER DOG

I used to have a cocker spaniel that was afraid of thunder. Whenever a thunderstorm came along, Sandy would put her head down and run around the edge of the yard, barking. So, in addition to being fearful, she wound up cold, wet, and completely consumed in behavior that had no meaning.

I was never afraid of thunder, because I knew the God of thunder. I understood that "it is His nature to be unchanging, constant, and completely trustworthy"[10]. I understood what thunder was about. I knew it was temporary and, ultimately, beneficial. I had peace about thunder my dog could never enjoy.

We cannot have peace about our identity and our destiny without knowing the God of our identity and destiny. We cannot enjoy the benefits God holds in His heart for us without knowing His heart. Only He can give us the freedom to become whom we were born to be. Without His guidance, we are consumed in behavior that has no meaning, on "a journey without an actual destination."[11]

Life as we were meant to experience it comes from knowing the Father. "Guidance is a by-product of a right relationship with God."[12]

---

10   Cooke, *Developing Your Prophetic Gifting*, p. 259.

11   Hamp, *Think Differently, Live Differently*, p. 54.

12   Cooke, *Developing Your Prophetic Gifting,* p. 198.

Only God could tell Gideon he was a mighty warrior. It is our birthright to hear God tell us whom He intended us to be. It is up to us to open our hearts to the work of the Holy Spirit. "May the God of hope fill you with all joy and peace as you trust in him, so that you may overflow with hope by the power of the Holy Spirit." (Romans 15:13) There can be no hope without power.

God has planted dreams in us. These dreams point us toward our destinies. "Yet, if we were honest with ourselves, the church would be the last place most people would go to have their dreams nurtured, developed, and unleashed.[13] This has to change. What can we do when our dreams seem so far away? "There are two possibilities open to us when God is not blessing us. We can either settle for the status quo, or we can cry to God."[14]

Cry out to God. That's what Gideon did. Crying out to God is the universal answer for people in the middle of nowhere. We may be assured of one thing: "Then you will call, and the Lord will answer; you will cry for help and he will say, 'Here am I.'" (Isaiah 58:9)

Crying out to God means that the status quo is no longer acceptable. It means we are ready and asking for change. But change is difficult. It requires surrender.

Let's not be like the Israelites who shrank back from God to maintain control. That only dooms us to stay the same, to stay trapped, to set up camp in the wilderness.

And remember, there are always two voices. "Satan speaks words into your mind of failure, defeat, hopelessness,

---

13   McManus, *The Barbarian Way*, p. 102.

14   Virgo, *Men of Destiny*, p. 75.

inability.... He delights in you seeing yourself as ordinary and unable to experience godly change."[15]

*H*OPE THAT REALLY MATTERS

Hope only for the future is unbiblical. Real hope makes a difference *now*.

Jesus was a difference maker. How did He do it? He stated plainly that He could do only what He saw the Father doing. In other words, He could align himself only with what the Father was already doing in someone's life. That is the ultimate purpose of enlightenment. Only when we see what the Father is ready to do in someone can we align ourselves with Him to empower that thing to happen. We must love with His hands, see with His eyes, and operate from His perspective. Only the empowerment of the Holy Spirit can enable such a miracle.

The Spirit does not come to give us strength; He *is* our strength. He does not come to give us victory; He *is* our victory. The Spirit does not come to take sides; He comes to take over.[16] Our only alternative is surrender. We present our bodies to Him as living sacrifices. He does His will through us. This is true worship.

✳ ✟ ✳

---

15   Bevere, *Extraordinary,* p. 182.

16   Thomas, *The Saving Life of Christ and The Mystery of Godliness*, pp. 129, 130.

CHAPTER 8

THE SWORD
of GIDEON

It's in Christ that we find out who we are and what we are living for.
Long before we first heard of Christ and got our hopes up, he had
his eye on us, had designs on us for glorious living, part of the overall
purpose he is working out in everything and everyone....

EPHESIANS 1:11-12, *The Message*

ᴅɪᴠɪɴᴇ ᴅᴇꜱᴛɪɴʏ

Erwin Raphael McManus tells the story of a young man in Los Angeles—we'll call him Dave—who accepted Christ and was subsequently scheduled to be baptized in the Pacific Ocean. An athletic type who aspired to play in the National Football League, Dave was terrified by the idea of going into the ocean. His fear stemmed from a childhood trauma. At the age of 11 he had witnessed a vicious shark attack on one of his friends. Years later, Dave's deathly fear of sharks persisted.

Not wanting to give the young man the easy way out by baptizing him in a pool or spa, McManus reasoned with him that if God spared Dave from the sharks it would indicate he had a destiny to fulfill. Dave decided to go through with it, even though he was still petrified. After being immersed and making it safely back to shore, Dave collapsed in the sand and began to weep. When asked whether it was out of fear or relief, he replied it was neither. Dave's tears stemmed from the realization that God had a purpose for his life.[1]

Dave was fortunate to learn this powerful lesson early in his Christian walk. Most of us have bought into the myth that God uses only a select few to accomplish His purposes. Feeling we are not among the chosen, we sit by the phone and watch the "on hold" button blink, waiting for God to call us to heaven. But God never intended for us to spend our time on earth waiting to die. Our lives mean as much to Him as anyone else's.

"Purposeful" is the opposite of "meaningless." God has a plan for each of us, designs on us for glorious living. But it is easy to lose sight of that in the daily grind of life and in the cultural currents that strive to push us out to sea.

How did Gideon move from the middle of nowhere to...getting somewhere?

> The angel of the Lord came...where Gideon was threshing wheat in a winepress to keep it from the Midianites. When the angel of the Lord appeared to Gideon, he said, "The Lord is with you, mighty warrior.... Go in the strength you have and save Israel out of Midian's hand. Am I not sending you?"
>
> "But Lord," Gideon asked, "How can I save Israel? My clan is the weakest in Manasseh, and I am the weakest in my family."
>
> The Lord answered, "I will be with you, and you will strike down the Midianites as if they were but one

---

1   McManus, *The Barbarian Way*, p. 97-98.

man." ... And the angel of the Lord disappeared. When
Gideon realized that it was the angel of the Lord, he
exclaimed, "Ah, Sovereign Lord! I have seen the angel of
the Lord face to face!"

But the Lord said to him, "Peace! Do not be afraid. You
are not going to die." (Judges 6:11-16, 22-23, NIV)

You are Not Who You Think You Are

Gideon saw himself as weak and insignificant. When he looked
at the circumstances around him, he was overwhelmed. He
had only one sword and the Midianites were a vast horde. It
seemed impossible for one man to make a difference in such a
tough situation. For most of us, it still seems that way today.

Where do these thoughts come from—these feelings of
hopelessness and insignificance? They come from a void deep
in our hearts. They stem from our failure to be the persons
God had in mind when He created us.[2]

Gideon had lost sight of his identity in God and of his
inheritance in the land of Canaan. He was skeptical, lacking
faith that God would deliver his people. He demonstrated the
fear passed down from Mount Sinai that an encounter with
God could be deadly. He was soon to learn, however, that he
was wrong on every count.

It must have shocked Gideon for the angel to address him
as "mighty warrior." But these two words from God marked
the beginning of a remarkable transformation that would
radically change the course of Gideon's life. Gideon would
discover he was not the person he thought he was. Instead,
he was the man God declared him to be. Gideon's journey to

2   Ortberg, *The Life You've Always Wanted,* p.13.

his destiny began when he accepted his true name. He was a mighty warrior.

God has placed something significant—a part of the revelation of Himself—inside each one of us. No one else can present this exact aspect of God's personality to the world. His earnest desire is to see us rise up and fulfill our destinies in Him.

Only God knows exactly why He created us. Only He knows our real name. We are who God says we are. But until we hear Him say it, we can only live shadow lives. If we are to move into our destinies, He must give us ears to hear His voice.

"When God calls you by name, it goes deeper than anything. It prepares you for the things God has prepared for you. But it is a battle to believe—especially for ourselves."[3]

*T*HE LORD IS PEACE

On the way to finding his destiny, Gideon also learned something about God. He found out God's presence is safe, not dangerous. It is a refuge of peace, not a place of death. Acting upon this new revelation, Gideon built an altar, calling it, "The Lord is Peace." We can build the proper kind of altar only if we have an accurate understanding of the nature of our God.

If only we could see what Gideon saw. He saw who the Lord really was, not through stories about the past, but through a present, personal experience. He discovered a God who was near, one who could make Himself small in order to talk to a man. He found a caring God, not an angry, vindictive taskmaster out to vaporize him.

---

3 Mary Forsythe, *Solving the Identity Crisis*, Gateway Church, May 6, 2006.

Encountering God fanned the flames of passion in Gideon's life. It brought hope for transformation. His identity opened the way to his destiny. He was a mighty warrior. Warriors have a purpose. "Go in the strength you have and save Israel out of Midian's hand."

At first, Gideon doubted, asking for a sign. He needed some encouragement in light of his circumstances. God gave it to him. This strengthened his faith. It created a sense of expectation that God might actually do something.

Think about the power of this encounter. Gideon had spoken with God and had lived to tell about it. He had been given a new sense of hope and vision. He had been given a new identity and had been commissioned to recapture his inheritance. He was empowered to take back what the Midianites had stolen. He was ready to fight for what was already his by divine birthright. In doing so he would see the power of God operate like he had never seen before. Gideon was moving from wimp to warrior to wow!

Our lives are similar powerhouses of possibility. Imagine the joy and satisfaction of "discovering your divine destiny and knowing for the first time who you were created to become."[4] Through the internal work of the Holy Spirit, Simons become Peters, Sauls become Pauls, and we become the people God had in mind when He made us.

TEAR DOWN YOUR FATHER'S IDOLS

Before he could move into God's purpose for his life, Gideon had business to take care of. "That same night the Lord said to him, 'Take the second bull from your father's herd, the one

---

4 McManus, *The Barbarian Way*, p. 104.

seven years old. Tear down your father's altar to Baal and cut
down the Asherah pole beside it. Then build a proper kind of
altar to the Lord your God on the top of this height." (Judges
6: 25-26)

Before Gideon could move forward with God, he had some
"homework" to take care of. We all do. Gideon's homework
involved a public demonstration of who or what was worthy
of his worship. And this was no small task. God told Gideon
to tear down his father's idols, *using his father's bull*. In
doing so, Gideon would be putting his very life on the line.
He would also be declaring, for all to see, "God is God, and
I will serve no other."

God is the only perfect father. Every other father has left
some kind of baggage for his children. For those who did not
have good fathers, it might be a history of abuse or a legacy
of addiction. For others, it could be the handicap of a poor
self-image or of feeling abandoned or unloved. Behind each
of these problems there is a spiritual stronghold or idol that
needs to be torn down. Gideon's father had made his god
too small. He had passed on the legacy of "The Lord will do
nothing" by turning to idols as his source of hope.

Most of us in America have also had our God made too
small. We don't expect Him to do much, especially for little
ol' insignificant us. But we do not have to be shackled by the
legacy of our fathers. Sooner or later, God will bring us to a
crossroads. We will reach the point of deciding for ourselves
whether or not to go on with God. Only we can tear down
our father's altars and idols. Only God can show us how.

What is the proper kind of altar to build in place of the
old ones? An altar is for worship and for sacrifice. In the Old
Testament it was a place for offering a sacrificial lamb. But

Jesus became the spotless lamb offered once and for all to atone for our sin. Do we now need altars at all?

Yes. The price has been paid for our salvation. No more sacrifice is needed for our sin. But we still have lives to live. To make our lives count for something, we need to live them in such a way as to please the Father. This is how God wants us to live. "Therefore, I urge you, brothers and sisters, in view of God's mercy, to offer your bodies as a living sacrifice, holy and pleasing to God—this is your true and proper worship." (Romans 12:1)

Worship is a declaration of whom or what is worthy of our love and devotion. It's not a one-time decision; it's a way of life.

Gideon's encounter with God caused him to change the object of his worship. It changed his power source, and it changed his purpose. Worship is living each day of our lives for the purpose of pleasing God, not ourselves.

Gideon decided to go on with God. He made the decision to obey the voice of the Lord, no matter the cost. Because of his obedience, he was able to see the God of wonders operate in his generation. Using Gideon and his army of only 300 men, God routed an army as "thick as locusts" and with camels that "could no more be counted than the sand on the seashore." (Judges 7:12)

Go Down Against the Camp

On the night of the battle, Gideon struggled with fear. God knew this and was faithful to encourage him. "During the night the Lord said to Gideon, 'Get up, go down against the camp, because I am going to give it into your hands. If you are afraid to attack, go down to the camp with your servant

Purah and listen to what they are saying. Afterward, you will be encouraged to attack the camp.'" (Judges 7: 9-11)

Having faith does not mean we will never be afraid. It means we will overcome our fears. We know Gideon was afraid, because he took God up on His offer and went down to the camp. As soon as he arrived, he overheard one Midianite sharing a dream with his friend. "A round loaf of barley bread came tumbling into the Midianite camp. It struck the tent with such force that the tent overturned and collapsed." (Judges 7:13)

On hearing the dream, "His friend responded, 'This can be nothing other than the sword of Gideon, son of Joash, the Israelite. God has given the whole camp into his hands.'" (Judges 7:14) The same sword that had leaned uselessly against the winepress wall was now a threat to the entire Midianite camp.

Upon hearing the dream and its interpretation, Gideon worshipped God. He returned to the camp of Israel and led them to the rout of the Midianites. Gideon thus fulfilled his calling and saved Israel from the hand of Midian.

*G*ETTING SOMEWHERE

I love two things about the story of Gideon. The first is watching the transformation that takes place in Gideon under God's gentle hand. The second thing I love is that God *knew* Gideon, and that he knew his life in detail. He was not a disconnected God, distanced from His children by time and space. He knew Gideon was alone and discouraged in the winepress. He knew that his father's second bull was seven years old. He even knew when Gideon was afraid. He knew everything about Gideon—all his faults and all his doubts—and He still loved him.

This is a story about the nature of God. He dealt with Gideon patiently and in loving kindness to bring him into His will.

WHAT IS IN YOUR HAND?

Gideon began his journey hindered by his father's mistakes, filled with doubt and fear, and unsure of his own identity. But he made a simple decision that completely changed the course of his life. It was the decision to trust the Lord and to obey Him at all cost.

You may be thinking, "That's great for Gideon, but he was a warrior even though he didn't know it. I'm definitely not a warrior. I really am a nobody. I don't even own a sword."

Neither did Moses.

After Moses fled from Egypt, he wound up in the desert in the middle of nowhere in a place called Midian. Moses had once believed he might be the man to deliver the Israelites from Egyptian slavery. Raised in Pharaoh's palace, he received the best education Egypt had to offer. Grieved at the oppression of his people, one day he struck an Egyptian taskmaster and killed him. He thought the Israelites would accept him as their leader, rise up, and throw off their chains.

Instead, he was chased into the wilderness where he had every reason to question his destiny. After herding sheep for 40 years, he must have believed the Lord had long since forgotten him.

Then Moses had an encounter with God in which God said, "I am sending you to Pharaoh to bring my people the Israelites out of Egypt." (Exodus 3:10) Moses, certain that his moment had long since passed, argued with God. "Who am I, that I should go?" (Exodus 3:11) "What if they do not believe me or listen to me?" (Exodus 4:1)

Look carefully at God's response. "What is that in your hand?" (Exodus 4:2) Since Moses was a shepherd, he carried a shepherd's staff. But when God told Moses to throw it on the ground, it became a snake. This would be a sign for Pharaoh. In Egypt, Moses also held his staff out to bring on the plagues. Later, he used it to part the Red Sea, to provide water for the people, and even to help them win battles.

THE PURPOSES OF GOD

God will not ask us to become something that is unnatural or foreign to us. Instead, He will ask us to become the person He created us to be. Each of us has something in his or her hand. It may not be a literal thing—it might be some kind of knowledge or a special gift or talent. It may seem as insignificant as a shepherd's staff.

Perhaps, as in the case of Moses, it has not dawned on us that we could be anything different from what we are. We are always in danger of resigning ourselves to our bad little jobs in the desert where we try to be average—content in life as spiritual nonentities.[5] But the story of Moses and the story of Gideon can be your story and mine. "Having received grace from God...we can enter into the fuller purposes of God for our lives and destiny in Christ, setting about certain tasks or 'works' that God has prepared specifically for us to do."[6]

---

5 *The Saving Life of Christ*, p. 65.

6 Hayford, *Grounds for Living*, p. 110.

MIGHTY WARRIORS

Of all the people in Israel during the time of the Midianite oppression, God chose Gideon to save Israel. He chose him because He knew him. He knew that, in spite of his faults, Gideon would hear, believe, and obey. He asks no more and no less of us.

The Lord is looking for mighty warriors—Christians who will listen to His voice and step out into their destinies. Satan is loath for this to happen, so this has been one of the key areas in which he has attacked the church. Satan has convinced many sincere and devoted Christians that God no longer speaks. His successful attacks in this area have robbed many Christians of their power and purpose.

Fortunately, God does still speak, and we can train our ears to hear Him. We can and we must, for this is the key to our destinies.

INHERITANCE

CHAPTER 9

A BETTER COVENANT

Enoch walked with God.

GENESIS 5:24, NIV, 1995

WALKING WITH GOD

"Then the man and his wife heard the sound of the Lord God as he was walking in the garden in the cool of the day, and they hid from the Lord God among the trees of the garden. But the Lord God called to the man, 'Where are you?'" (Genesis 3:9)

So begins the strange story of the first encounter between God and Adam and Eve after the couple had eaten from the tree of the knowledge of good and evil. I'm not a rocket scientist, but it seems to me that there is a back-story here. Apparently God frequently showed up in Eden during the cool of the day with His walking shoes on. Evidently Adam and Eve were in the habit of meeting God there and joining Him on His strolls through the garden He had created.

What would it be like to walk with God, and is that something we should know? Does this fall into the twilight zone of theology, or is there an understandable answer to the question?

Let's start with some basic observations.

Adam and Eve owned the first garden home. That's because God created it and then gave it to them to live in and to tend. (Genesis 2:15) Once God and Adam got all the animals named and God created Eve, it seems God visited the garden once or maybe twice a day when it was pleasant and cool. (Pardon me if all my observations don't come with explanations.)

Did God create man to tend the garden or so He could walk with him in the cool of the day? God didn't need a garden, and He didn't need someone to tend it. God made man so He could walk with him.

He created you and me for the same reason. He formed us for fellowship and love. That's why He created us in His own image, not in the image of a tomato-harvesting robot.

Then Adam and Eve sinned, and God banished them from the garden. Not from His presence, but from the garden. Remember, it was their home, not His.

God had a perfectly sound and, in fact, loving reason for banning them from the garden. It still contained the tree of life. (Genesis 3:22-24) If Adam and Eve had eaten from that tree in their fallen state, they would have been doomed to live that way forever.

All that being said, let's get back to the question. Why don't we know what it would it be like to walk with God? Maybe it's because all this time we have made the wrong assumption about God. Does He want to walk with us or not? We can answer this question by looking at some of God's people.

ENOCH WALKED WITH GOD

"And Enoch walked with God; then he was no more, because God took him away." (Genesis 5:24, NIV, 1995) This scripture flies in the face of everything we have accepted as the experience of fallen man. Enoch walked with the Lord, just as Adam walked with Him in the Garden of Eden. God and Enoch had an intimate relationship. They became so close, in fact, that one day God "took him away" so that he did not experience death.

"Noah was a just man, perfect among his generations. Noah walked with God." (Genesis 6:9) Maybe it was while they were walking together that God spoke to Noah and gave him the blueprint for an ark in which he and his family were saved from the flood.

God appeared to Abraham on several occasions and even called him His friend. (James 2:23) Jacob wrestled with God, then built an altar on that spot saying he had seen God "face to face." (Genesis 32:30).

Concerning Moses, we are told, "The Lord would speak to Moses face to face, as a man speaks with his friend." (Exodus 33:11)

These men, as well as Gideon, David, and Elijah, lived under a covenant that was inferior to the one we live under today. (Hebrews 7:22, 8:6) Yet their experience of God was more intimate and more powerful than most of us would ever dream of. Even in the Old Testament, God could be known. "You will seek me and find me when you seek me with all your heart." (Jeremiah 29:13)

Unfair Advantage

It used to seem to me that the men of the Bible had an advantage over men of today. The disciples walked with Jesus, and not just in the cool of the day. In the Old Testament, God — or His angels — appeared to men and spoke with them.

This seemed unfair to me. Surely I could have their kind of faith if I had a face-to-face encounter with God, Jesus, or an angel. I felt like an orphan because I had a poor understanding of God's heart toward us and of the way He reveals himself to us today.

My church only added to the confusion. I was taught that God reveals himself to us now only through the Bible. Our new and better covenant, I was told, consists totally of the completed work of Jesus and the written word of God.

This is a common teaching. Even in seminary, one author notes, theology "exchanged the mystical and miraculous for doctrine and ritual. What the Spirit once did, programs have now replaced, and even the Scriptures themselves became proof that God had stopped speaking."[1]

Don't get me wrong: I am grateful beyond words for the redemptive work of Jesus. He took the full punishment for our sins and paid the full price for our salvation. There is nothing we can do to put God in our debt or to earn heaven. God does not want us to live as if we owe Him something. He wants us to live as if we love Him.

Furthermore, I believe that the Bible is the complete and inerrant word of God. I love and need the Bible, but I love and need God more. I would rather take golf lessons from Arnold Palmer than read 10 books he wrote on the subject. That's why I want to walk with God. I think He knows a thing or two about His book.

*N*O RESPECTER OF PERSONS

Did God reveal himself to the great men of the Bible because

---

1 McManus, *The Barbarian Way,* p. 77.

of a special office He had for them or because they lived in a special time when God's power and presence were needed more than they are today? Or was there some other special quality they shared?

Since God is no respecter of persons, let's assume for a moment that God offers all men an equal opportunity to walk with Him. Let's assume that He loves us just as much as He loved them and that His presence and power are there for us to enjoy now just as much as they were then. That would mean that there was something else that drew God to these men and caused Him to favor them. We would be wise to know what that quality is and whether or not it is available to us today.

It is not a great mystery. The book of Hebrews tells us exactly what set these men apart:

> By faith Enoch was taken from this life, so that he did not experience death; he could not be found, because God had taken him away. For before he was taken, he was commended as one who pleased God. And without faith it is impossible to please God, because anyone who comes to God must believe that he exists and that he rewards those who earnestly seek him.
>
> By faith Noah, when warned about things not yet seen, in holy fear built an ark to save his family. By his faith he condemned the world and became heir of the righteousness that is in keeping with faith.
>
> By faith Abraham, when called to go to a place he would later receive as his inheritance, obeyed and went, even though he did not know where he was going. By faith he made his home in the promised land like a stranger in a foreign country; he lived in tents, as did Isaac and Jacob, who were heirs with him of the same promise....

> By faith, Jacob, when he was dying, blessed each of Joseph's sons, and worshipped as he leaned on the top of his staff....
>
> By faith [Moses] left Egypt, not fearing the king's anger; he persevered because he saw him who is invisible." (Hebrews 11:5-9, 21, 27)

These were not twilight-zone men. They did not live in a different world or a special time or place. They were all men "just like us." Only one thing was exceptional about them: they exhibited exceptional faith. They heard and obeyed God.

We tend to put these men on a pedestal and think we could never attain such faith. Fortunately, there is another person listed in Hebrews to help put our minds at rest: "By faith the prostitute Rahab, because she welcomed the spies, was not killed with those who were disobedient." (Hebrews 11:31) Rahab was not even an Israelite, yet she is listed with Enoch, Abraham, and Moses because of her faith.

SOMETHING BETTER FOR US

The author of Hebrews was speaking of a faith that is available to everyone. "And without faith it is impossible to please God, because anyone who comes to God must believe that he exists and that he rewards those who earnestly seek him." (Hebrews 11:6)

It was neither the position occupied by these people nor the dispensation in which they lived that was special, it was their faith. God is looking for people who trust Him enough to seek Him passionately, and He promises to reward them with His presence.

If we want what was normal for these people of faith to be normal for us, we must elevate our faith to a radical new level. God wants us to seek Him rather than wait around for Him. We will never find the knowledge of God or the fullness of Christ as long as we are locked into a spiritual culture that expects the Lord to do nothing.

God's word declares our lives should outshine the lives of Enoch, Abraham, Moses, and Rahab. "These were all commended for their faith, yet none of them received what had been promised, since God had planned something better for us so that only together with us would they be made perfect." (Hebrews 6:39-40) Either we must change our beliefs to conform to what God says or we must accept the hard, cold fact that the Bible is not really true—not for us, not today.

Our Better Covenant

Our covenant truly is better. This statement even comes with an eternal lifetime guarantee. "Jesus has become the guarantee of a better covenant." (Hebrews 7:22, NIV) Since Jesus is alive and well and seated at the right hand of God, He is still the guarantee of a better covenant.

If you listen to some people, our covenant changed after the apostles died and the word of God was unified into the Bible. They want you to believe in a new covenant "A," for back then, and a new covenant "B" that we live under now. They say that now that the church is firmly established and we have the Bible in its entirety, our covenant no longer includes miracles, encounters with God, or even the ability to hear His voice.

Nowhere in the Bible will you find anything about new covenant "A" and new covenant "B." In fact, there is much the Bible says to the contrary. The author of Hebrews tells us, "Now may the God of peace, who through the blood of the eternal covenant brought back from the dead our Lord Jesus, that great shepherd of the sheep, equip you with everything good for doing his will, and may he work in us what is pleasing to him, through Jesus Christ, to whom be glory forever and ever." (Hebrews 13:20)

This scripture tells us two things about the new covenant: first, it is eternal; second, it is ratified by blood.

ETERNAL

An eternal covenant is, well...eternal. Eternal means from now on—from this point forward forever. There can be no covenant that comes after an eternal covenant. Our new covenant cannot go away, diminish, or change.

That means every promise of the new covenant applies just as much to us as it ever did to anyone else. We should accept the idea that God still speaks. We should expect the miraculous indwelling of the Holy Spirit. We should be open to miracles, healing, dreams, visions, and every other wonderful thing God has promised. "For no matter how many promises God has made, they are 'Yes' in Christ." (2 Corinthians 1:20)

God's promises don't go away. They never expire. The "Yes" is forever.

We are in Christ, now and forever. That should get us excited. God never intended for *Monday Night Football* to be more exciting than living life. He didn't call us to be second-class citizens under a second-class covenant, doomed to hiding in our dens while we wait for the second coming. If we don't rise up to fulfill our destiny, another generation will. It happened to the Israelites and it could happen to us. But it doesn't have to.

Ratified by Blood

Biblical covenants were ratified by blood. In the Old Testament, covenants were usually consummated by cutting an animal in half. The participants would then walk between the two halves of the animal to seal the deal. (Jeremiah 34:18-19) The blood of the animal served to ratify the covenant and was called the blood of the covenant. (Exodus, 24:8, Zechariah 9:11, Hebrews 9:20)

Jesus ratified the new covenant with His blood. During the last supper, He took the cup of communion and stated, "This is my blood of the covenant, which is poured out for many." (Matthew 26:28, Mark 14:24) Jesus' blood is the blood of the eternal covenant. For the new covenant to be replaced, to ever change, or to ever have changed, Jesus would have to shed His blood. He would have to die again. But He died once and for all (Romans 6:10) and He cannot die again. (Romans 6:9) Our new covenant is as sure and as permanent as the blood of Jesus Christ.

Better Promises

The new covenant is a better covenant because it is ratified by the blood of Jesus rather than the blood of bulls and goats, which could never take away sin. (Hebrews 10:4) It is also founded on better promises, "But in fact the ministry Jesus has received is as superior to theirs [the Old Testament priests] as the covenant of which he is the mediator is superior to the old one, since the new covenant is established on better promises." (Hebrews 8:6)

If we want to live in fullness of life, and if we want to glorify Jesus on this earth, we need to know, accept, and walk in all the promises of our new and better covenant. The promises are ours for the taking, and they are better than we could ever ask for or imagine.

Let's start with four promises from the book of Jeremiah. "'This is the covenant I will make with the house of Israel after that time,' declares the Lord. 'I will put my law in their minds and write it on their hearts. I will be their God, and they will be my people. No longer will they teach their neighbor, or say to one another, "Know the Lord," because they will all know me, from the least of them to the greatest,' declares the Lord. 'For I will forgive their wickedness and will remember their sins no more.'" (Jeremiah 31:31-34)

These are amazing promises:

+ *I will put my law in their minds and write it on their hearts.* This does not mean we will be better able to memorize the Ten Commandments so that we will "know them by heart." It signifies a change from an external set of rules to an internal guidance system that will lead us to walk in God's ways and according to His principles.

+ *I will be their God, and they will be my people.* We will be a people who are identified with God, bearing His name and bringing glory to Him.

+ *They will all know me.* Each of us will have the ability to have an active, meaningful connection with the Father, relating to Him on an individual basis.

+ *I will forgive their wickedness and will remember their sins no more.* There will "be once and for all" forgiveness for sin that provides for fellowship with God now and even more complete fellowship with Him one day in heaven.

Better promises should produce better hope within us. (Hebrews 7:18-19) The old covenant is weak and useless compared to the new and better covenant Jesus put in place for us. The new covenant gives us hope that we can be close to God in this lifetime.

A Covenant-Making God

God is a covenant-making and a covenant-keeping God. The Bible tells us about a series of covenants God has made with men. Each covenant contains certain behaviors God required of men along with certain promises from God for those who were faithful to live by His requirements.

God first made a covenant with Adam and Eve, then with Noah, and then with Abraham, Isaac, and Jacob. But the Old Testament is mostly about the covenant God made with the children of Israel at Mount Sinai based on the Law of Moses. The New Testament tells about the new and better covenant based on the redeeming work of Jesus.

But we don't have a very good grasp of that concept today. We seem to have trouble seeing just how different the old and new covenants are. So let's put it another way. The Old Testament is about an antiquated and ineffective way of relating to God which was based on law and performance and which could not and did not work because of the frailty of man. The New Testament is about a completely new and radical way of relating to God as a person and not through a religious system.

Under the new covenant we operate from a position of grace. It is based on the free gift of the righteousness of Christ that gives us access to God and allows us to live in an active and growing relationship with Him as we are led and empowered by the Holy Spirit. It's not just about going to heaven—it's about knowing and walking with God.

So why do so many people seem to want to go back to relating to God based on various sets of laws, rules, traditions, and/or denominational doctrines by which it is impossible to reach God? I believe it is for the same reason the children of Israel did not want God to speak to them at Mount Sinai. Hearing God is dangerous. It gives Him the power to intrude into our lives. If we hear Him we are compelled to obey. To follow rules, we don't have to engage our hearts.

But our hearts are exactly what God wants. "There is absolutely no biblical expectation of a gospel without power, of a religion without spiritual experience, of doctrine and morals without divine encounter."[2]

A CHRISTMAS STORY

One year my parents gave me an airplane for Christmas. It was a scale model of the U.S. Navy Corsair used during World War II. It had a liquid-fueled engine that propelled the fighter plane so that you could fly it in a circle on the end of a string.

I loved my awesome new fighter. I could hardly wait to fly it. But we never did. My parents had spent a lot of money on my gift and didn't want me to crash it. We started the engine once, but my beautiful navy-blue airplane never flew.

God has given us the most precious gift in the world. It is more than the gift of salvation; it is the gift of the ability to know Him. (Jeremiah 24:7) This gift is the most costly gift ever given — the price for it was the life of Jesus Christ. Imagine God's disappointment when, day after day, we leave this gift in the box. A gift that is never used is worse than no gift at all.

---

2   Alan Smith, *Unveiled* (Fort Worth, TX: Authority Press, 2011), p. 47.

We must be bold to take advantage of the riches God has lavished on us. Satan knows this and attacks us with fear. What if we fail? What if we crash and burn? What if we are not worthy? What if God is mad at us?

These are not the real issues, because Satan is a liar. The price for our failures has already been paid. We have received the righteousness of Christ and have been made worthy through Him. God is a loving Father, not an angry tyrant. The desire of God's heart is for intimacy with us. Only our sinful, unbelieving hearts can turn us away from the living God. (Hebrews 3:12)

Ears to Hear

We have heard God's call, and we can hear Him again. We have the opportunity to enjoy our Christmas present every day. We can take it out of the box and enjoy a relationship with God that is deeper and better than Enoch's, Gideon's, or David's.

But we have been hindered by our culture of unbelief. The constant chatter of our society does not teach us to listen to quiet voices like the gentle whisper of God. (1 Kings 19:12) The busy-ness of our culture prevents us from taking the time to listen to the small, still internal witness of the Holy Spirit. Still, "The Holy Spirit has much to say if we learn to listen. He is the means to all revelation from God."[3]

God will not shout to get our attention. He wants us to freely give it to Him out of a willing, humble, and obedient heart. This was David's heartfelt cry: "Teach me to do your will, for you are my God; may your good Spirit lead me on level ground." (Psalm 143:10)

---

3   Sheets, *Watchman Prayer*, p. 153.

There is in our time a quiet desperation to hear God and to know His direction for our lives. Our silent longings for His guidance need not go unanswered if we are willing to take the long and sometimes difficult road that so many leave untraveled. We must train our ears to hear.

"Much of the adventure of Christian living involves responsiveness to the guidance of the Holy Spirit."[4] Today is the day to hear God's voice. (Hebrews 3:7) Guidance always follows surrender.

A Covenant of the Spirit

"'As for me, this is my covenant with them,' says the Lord. 'My Spirit, who is on you, will not depart from you, and my words that I have put in your mouth, will always be on your lips, on the lips of your children, and on the lips of their descendants—from this time on and forever,' says the Lord." (Isaiah 59:21)

The new covenant is an everlasting covenant (Hebrews 13:20), and the promise of the Holy Spirit under that covenant is from this time on and forever. An everlasting covenant has no end. There can never be a new covenant "B" under which the Holy Spirit goes into exile. If there were, its promises would be clearly set forth in scripture.

The new covenant is a covenant of the Spirit. "This is a covenant not of written laws, but of the Spirit. The old written covenant ends in death; but under the new covenant, the Spirit gives life." (2 Corinthians 3:6, NLT) The Holy Spirit is so central to the new covenant that it would not be the new covenant without Him.

---

4   Ortberg, *The Life You've Always Wanted,* p. 155.

The Curtain is Torn

Salvation is not the end result of accepting Christ; it is the starting point of abundant life. It's what puts us into the position of being able to come to the Father. Making it all about salvation is just another way of making the gift more important than the Giver.

The Bible makes this clear, but we seem to be awfully forgetful about it. If Christ died for a reason, maybe the thing that happened at the moment He died is something we need to pay attention to. Perhaps it has special significance. Immediately upon His death the curtain of the temple was torn in two, from top to bottom. The way was opened into the Holy of Holies. (Matthew 27:50-51, Mark 15:37-38)

I don't always catch on to symbolism, but this was a big deal. The temple was God's dwelling place. The people came from all over Israel to worship Him there. But only the high priest could go into the Holy of Holies because God's presence was there. The place was so holy that even the high priest could enter only once a year. The penalty for anyone violating this prohibition was immediate death.

But Jesus died in our place. The curtain was torn.

Entering the Holy of Holies

In one earth-shattering moment the way was opened. The barrier between God and man was removed. "The former regulation is set aside because it was weak and useless (for the law made nothing perfect), and a better hope is introduced, by which we draw near to God." (Hebrews 7:18-19)

Since the curtain has been torn, the temple is no longer necessary. We are His new dwelling place. "Know you not that your bodies are the temple of the Holy Spirit, who is in you, whom you have received from God? You are not your own; you were bought at a price. Therefore honor God with your bodies." (1 Corinthians 6:19-20)

The Holy Spirit can now live in us because we were purchased by God. He paid a great price, not just to save us but to redeem everything about us—our bodies, souls and spirits, our identities, and His purpose for our lives. Everything has changed.

Anyone who offers a form of hope that is not based on drawing near to God and being filled with the Holy Spirit is offering an inferior hope. The Spirit activates the ways of God within us, and we spill out His goodness on those around us. "Whoever believes in me, as the scripture has said, rivers of living water will flow from within them. By this he meant the Spirit...." (John 7:38-39a)

The Holy Spirit is the gift without which the new covenant would not be new. Through Him we have become "ministers of the new covenant, not of the letter [the law] but of the Spirit; for the letter kills, but the Spirit gives life." (2 Corinthians 3:6, NKJV) We have moved from the ministry of condemnation to the ministry of righteousness. (2 Corinthians 3:9)

Righteousness does not mean we are living right every moment of our lives, but that we have been set firmly and completely in right relationship with God. We are free to pursue Him without shame, without guilt, and without condemnation. We have a completely new way of relating to God. We are free to worship Him in Spirit and in truth.

Entering the Holy of Holies once a year did not offer hope enough for building a deep relationship with God. The future hope of heaven doesn't, either. We have a better hope, by which we draw near to God now. "Therefore brothers and sisters, since we have confidence to enter the Most Holy Place by the blood of Jesus, by a new and living way opened for us through the curtain, that is, his body…let us draw near to God." (Hebrews 10:19-22)

There, in the Most Holy Place, we come to understand and take on the character of God. Worship fulfills us and transforms us. It shows us who God is and reveals our identity in Him.

Elijah Was a Man Just Like Us

Suppose we were to actually believe Elijah was a man just like us. Suppose we were to accept everything God has for us: salvation through His son Jesus Christ, daily washing and renewal through the Bible, and intimacy with God that puts us in touch with His power through the indwelling of the Holy Spirit. Then we could say, "I am a man just like Elijah, only better. My normal really is better than his normal. I live in the middle of somewhere, in the middle of God's presence, His will, His power, and His destiny for my life. I am exactly where I need to be, and I wouldn't trade places with anyone in the world.

CHAPTER 10

THE PROMISE LAND

The Lord will establish you as his holy people,

as he promised you on oath....

(DEUTERONOMY 28:9A)

✐HE GOD OF THE PROMISES

When Gideon's god was too small, Gideon knew something was wrong with his life. Although he was where he was supposed to be physically—in the Promised Land—there didn't seem to be anything promising about it. It was just real estate, and the issue of who owned it appeared to be in doubt. Gideon lived in a vacuum in which the promises associated with the Promised Land were absent.

Let's have a look at those promises:

> You will be blessed in the city and blessed in the country. The fruit of your womb will be blessed, and the crops of your land and the young of your livestock—the calves of your herds and the lambs of your flocks.
>
> Your basket and your kneading trough will be blessed. You will be blessed when you come in and blessed when you go out.

The Lord will grant that the enemies who rise up against you will be defeated before you. They will come at you from one direction and flee from you in seven.

The Lord will send a blessing on your barns and on everything you put your hand to. The Lord your God will bless you in the land he is giving you.

The Lord will establish you as his holy people, as he promised you on oath, if you keep the commands of the Lord your God and walk in obedience to him. Then all the peoples on earth will see that you are called by the name of the Lord, and they will fear you.

The Lord will grant you abundant prosperity—in the fruit of your womb, the young of your livestock and the crops of your ground—in the land he swore to your ancestors to give you.

The Lord will open the heavens, the storehouse of his bounty, to send rain on your land in season and to bless the work of your hands. You will lend to many nations, but will borrow from none. The Lord will make you the head and not the tail." (Deuteronomy 28:3-13)

As we can see from this passage, the Lord wanted to give His people much more than land. I call it the "promise land" because it provided the setting in which God wanted to give His people every blessing He had in His heart for them.

The land was not an end in itself, rather the blessings of God were meant to be apprehended *in the land*. But all the blessings disappeared because Israel was serving the wrong god. When people stop serving the God of the promises, the promises slip away.

A DESOLATE INHERITANCE

As long as Gideon was unclear about who God was, he couldn't know who Gideon was either. Since Gideon didn't know his identity, he couldn't know what was his. As a result, he lived in a desolate inheritance. That is exactly where Satan wants us to live. If we don't understand what is ours, we will not properly defend it.

Satan is all about his unholy trinity of activities—killing, stealing, and destroying. (John 10:10) And there is nothing, other than our eternal salvation, that he would rather steal or destroy than our inheritance. So he works overtime to take away our promise land which, by the way, is not heaven. The promise land cannot represent heaven because the enemy was there and had to be driven out.

Satan is not allowed to just walk in and steal our inheritance, but he can try to get us to give it away. If we fail to understand what our inheritance is, or to see how precious it is, we may mishandle it and give up many of its benefits. The Bible offers several examples of how this can happen.

THE PRODIGAL SON

Two of these examples occur in the same parable—the story of the prodigal son. We have already looked at this story from the perspective of the father. Now, let's examine it from the perspective of his sons. There are two sons in the story, and the lesson to be learned from each son is equally important.

"There was a man who had two sons. The younger one said to his father, 'Father, give me my share of the estate.' So he divided his property between them. Not long after that, the younger son got together all he had, set off for a distant country and there squandered his wealth on wild living." (Luke 15:11-13)

The prodigal son wanted his inheritance, and he didn't want to wait for it. Upon receiving it, the Bible tells us, he spent all the money on wild living, a reckless, hedonistic approach to life that put pleasure above all else. His message to the father was basically, "Hey, Dad, you have not died soon enough to suit me. Since you won't hurry up and die, just give me my money now. I have no desire to have relationship with you, and I have better things to do than stay here with you, down on the farm."

Since the father in the story represents God, we could say the prodigal left Him to serve another god, the god of pleasure. How many Americans claim to be Christians and yet serve this god? You hear them saying things like, "I know God wants me to be happy. That's why I'm leaving my wife, going all out for success, or buying myself a new car." Their "happiness" is the only thing that matters to them. It matters even more than God's will for their lives. This leads to lack of commitment, partial repentance, and willingness to serve other gods. The lack of desire to know God or fully pursue Him is evidence of just who is in charge of their lives.

The prodigal despised his inheritance because he didn't understand it. The fact that his father was not dead meant that *he still had a father*. All the benefits of sonship and of the father's house were his to enjoy, but his rebellious, selfish heart led him to throw it all away.

*T*HE ELDER BROTHER

The elder brother could have been the hero of this story, but he wasn't. The first sign of trouble was when the prodigal returned and the father joyfully received him with open arms (as God does for us). Rather than rejoicing with the father, the older son was judgmental and angry.

He lamented having served the father all his life and having never been given a fattened calf so he could party with his friends. Clearly, there had been no joy in it for him, either. He had served out of a sense of duty and obligation, looking only to his future inheritance for motivation. It was his desire to meet the minimum requirements of sonship only so that he would someday receive the inheritance he had worked so hard to earn.

Like his brother, the elder son had lost the joy of knowing the father. He lived his life from a sense of duty and obligation. "The dutiful do not experience the Father's embrace."[1] This produced an inability to receive the present benefits of the father's house. He served his father like a slave and not a son.

The elder brother represented the Pharisees of Jesus' day. They prided themselves in their knowledge of the scriptures and depended on their own righteousness in the works of the law to get them to heaven. They judged others and always thought of themselves as better than everybody else. One could argue that they served the gods of power and success. Jesus had no tolerance for the Pharisees, calling them snakes, whitewashed tombs, and other very uncomplimentary things. It appears that, at least in Jesus' day, "the 'righteous' were more damaged by their righteousness than the sinners were by their sin."[2]

I hope this is not reminding you of someone you know. Such a person today might be unhappy, judgmental, and difficult to like. They would be proud of their doctrine but lacking in the application of its compassion and love. Even so, hear the heart of the father as he invites his child to change his mind.

---

1   Eldredge, *The Journey of Desire,* p. 48.

2   Ortberg, *The Life You've Always Wanted,* p. 34.

"My son...you are always with me and everything I have is yours." (Luke 15:31)

Both the prodigal and his brother completely missed the point. Inheritance is, above all else, about right relationship with the father. The good news is that the younger son finally came to his senses. When the prodigal returned, he was richer than his brother. True, he had no money, but at least he knew who he was and who his father was. He knew there was blessing in his father's house and was able to receive all the father had to offer—not selfishly or out of duty or obligation, but based on love.

*T*HE STORY OF ESAU

The third biblical example of one who despised his inheritance is Esau. Jacob and Esau were the twin sons of Isaac and Rebecca. But Esau was born first and, therefore, had the birthright of the firstborn son. Under Jewish custom, this entitled him to receive the blessing of the father and the lion's share of the inheritance.

Esau was a "man's man" who loved to hunt and take care of himself. One could argue that he served the gods of independence and control. But one day he failed to kill anything and returned home famished. Jacob had a nice stew going, and Esau asked for some of it. Jacob, ever the schemer, told Esau he would trade a bowl of his stew for Esau's birthright. As incredible as it may seem, Esau accepted the bargain. In this way, he despised his birthright.

Esau despised his birthright because he thought he didn't need it. Priding himself on his independence, he figured he could take care of himself. The Bible is very hard on Esau, calling him godless. (Hebrews 12:16)

We live godlessly when we live independent of God, thinking we can do it on our own. We are the products of a society established on independence and self-sufficiency. America is the richest nation on earth. We enjoy the benefits of this wealth. We have food in the refrigerator, money in the bank, and health insurance. We're covered. Why do we need God?

THE BEST PART

Someday my sister and I will divide our inheritance. When that day comes I am confident that we would both give it all up to have our parents back. Their things will never mean as much to us as they have.

The greatest thing about having a future inheritance is that it means we have a father now. When we have a father we have:

* Relationship with someone who loves us and cares for us.

* An identity and a name.

* A place—his house—where we will always be welcome and always belong.

* A base—a place from which to operate and move forward.

If that is true of our earthly fathers, how much more is it true of God? Are we more interested in God or in what He can do for us? We can be hedonistic and want the blessing now. We can be legalistic and wait for the blessing in the future. We can be independent and try to arrange for our own blessing. Or we can turn our eyes to the Father and enjoy all the blessings of His house, both now and in the future.

Every inheritance has a now part and a future part. Many Christians look only on the greatness of the future part of our spiritual inheritance. Yes, heaven will be much better than earth, but we shouldn't despise the now part of our inheritance. We can know God today for who He is, not for what He owns. We have the opportunity for relationship with Him as our loving Father, not just as someone who will bless us someday. Without Him our promise land becomes the middle of nowhere.

David understood the idea that we have a now and a future inheritance. He declared:

* "Lord, you alone are my portion and my cup; you make my lot secure. The boundary lines have fallen for me in pleasant places; surely I have a delightful inheritance." (Psalm 16:5-6) If there were no heaven, knowing God now would be enough.

* "I cry out to God Most High, to God who will fulfill his purpose for me." (Psalm 57:2, NLT) We are here for a reason, and there is joy in fulfilling our purpose.

* "Those who know your name trust in you, for you, Lord, have never forsaken those who seek you." (Psalm 9:10) God has given us His name as part of our inheritance. We are part of His household. Knowing God is better than having stuff.

*T*HE BLESSINGS OF GOD'S HOUSE

When the prodigal son returned home, he had used up all his future inheritance. He understood the extent of his sin against his father and against their relationship. He was prepared to admit that he was no longer worthy to be called a son. He felt that the best he could hope for was life as a hired servant.

The father would have none of this. His son had returned and was fully restored to his position of sonship. Even so, the only blessings left for him were those which comprised his present inheritance. The now part of our inheritance is every blessing our Father God has in His heart to give us today.

> But the father said to his servants, "Quick! Bring the best
> robe and put it on him. Put a ring on his finger and sandals
> on his feet. Bring the fattened calf and kill it. Let's have a
> feast and celebrate. For this son of mine was dead and is
> alive again; he was lost and is found." (Luke 15:22-24)

The full extent of this blessing is revealed by each action the father took. These actions have the same significance for us as they did for the prodigal son.

First, our Father gave each of us a clean robe. This represents the robe of the righteousness of Christ we received at the moment of our salvation. Righteousness means right relationship with God. We can approach God, robed in the purity of Christ, any time, any day because of the sacrifice, once for all, of the Lamb of God. (Romans 6:10) "But now a righteousness from God, apart from the law, has been made known, to which the Law and the Prophets testify. This righteousness from God comes through faith in Jesus Christ to all who believe." (Romans 3:21-22, NLT)

Second, He placed on our finger the signet ring of His authority. This declares we are empowered to do business in His name. His throne is the base from which we operate. His full identity and all of His power stand behind us when we move under His authority. Nothing is impossible for us when we walk in obedience to Him. We can expect the supernatural because He is a supernatural being and because His name is behind everything we do.

Third, He has put on our feet the sandals of sonship. Only sons were given sandals because sandals would make it easier for a slave to run away. Our freedom is the freedom to worship, to be sons and daughters, and to be like our Father. It is the freedom to become all that He ever envisioned for us to be. We are free to move toward our destinies with the full assurance of His parental love and support.

Finally, He has killed the fattened calf in our honor. This feast is an affirmation that we are home. We have a place where we are welcome, celebrated and affirmed. God's presence is our home, and we can enter at any time without knocking.

He has invited us to feast and celebrate with our Father, the Son, and our brothers and sisters in the church. Just as He invited Israel to a sacred feast in the desert, He invites us to commune with Him in the presence of the saints.

This feast is yet another reminder that true freedom is found only in His presence. As the prodigal son discovered, any other freedom is false and ultimately destructive. False freedom promises but never delivers, feeds but never satisfies, and invites us to a life that appears to be exciting but that ultimately leads only to death.

The feast also reminds us that we are in this together. God gave different gifts to different people. The church needs all of its members in combination to represent the fullness of Christ. Each one of us is like a single facet of the beautiful diamond that represents Christ to the world. Any one of us who is not part of a body of believers is not representing Jesus to the world in the way the Father intended.

Our Father's Face

In his book, *Think Differently, Live Differently*, Bob Hamp tells the story of a different lost son, separated from his parents for many years without knowing that the people who raised him were not his parents. After being reunited with his real father and mother, he had an "aha" experience. "As he looked into his father's face, he saw himself. He saw his own eyes, his own cheekbones. He was staring into his birthright and his heritage."[3]

We are God's children. We carry His DNA. When we look at Him we find out who we are. If we lived according to our identity rather than what we are someday going to receive, we would act like sons, not slaves. A son knows how to please his father. We can know the pleasure of pleasing God.

God gave us the gift of Himself when He made us in His image. Then God gave us His Son. Through His act of redemption, we have been reborn into His image. Finally, God gives us His Spirit. By His power we are transformed into His image. (2 Corinthians 3:17) "When the Creator [indwells] his creation, there is transformation...[and] you are no longer suited for a normal life."[4]

OUR GLORIOUS INHERITANCE IN THE SAINTS

As has already been stated, Israel's inheritance was not just land. It consisted of the promises (or blessings) God wanted to give the Israelites. God, the source, wanted to pour out blessings on His chosen people, who were the object of His love. The land was simply a place for that to happen.

What is our inheritance? Our first clue is its location — in the saints. Israel's inheritance was in the land. Ours lies within our brothers and sisters. We are the Father's house and the place where His Spirit dwells. There are blessings available to us that can be apprehended only in and from each other. The church is the place for that to happen.

This may be shocking news to lone-ranger Christians. Avoiding the church because it is filled with imperfect people

3   Hamp, *Think Differently, Live Differently*, p. 129.

4   McManus, *The Barbarian Way*, p. 66.

is despising our inheritance. Living in this manner, according to the Bible, is living godlessly.

We have a treasure that can be apprehended only from jars of clay—the imperfect vessels who are God's people:

> For those who are led by the Spirit of God are the children of God. The Spirit you received does not make you slaves, so that you live in fear again; rather the Spirit you received brought about your adoption to sonship. And by him we cry, "*Abba*, Father." The Spirit himself testifies with our spirit that we are God's children. Now if we are children, then we are heirs—heirs of God and co-heirs with Christ. (Romans 8:14-17)

Our inheritance in not a physical place on earth. Our inheritance is every blessing the Father wants to give us in the family of God. We all share in the blessings of our new identity. In Christ we are given a robe of righteousness, the sandals of sonship, a signet ring of authority, an elder brother who loves us and intercedes for us, and the indwelling Holy Spirit to affirm and empower us.

The promised land was a place of blessing for a special people:

+ "The Lord will establish you as his holy people, as he promised you on oath....

+ Then all the peoples on earth will see that you are called by the name of the Lord....

+ And they will fear you." (Deuteronomy 28:3-13)

The blessings for God's people today are even greater than those for His people in the Old Testament. We live under the better promises of the new covenant. His desire is to establish us as His holy people, unique in all the earth. All nations should recognize that we are set apart to be called by the name of the only true and living God. As people who fear Him, we should command the awe of all people who do not. It can happen in this generation. All God is looking for is people who will believe and enter.

CHAPTER 11

GRAIN, NEW WINE, *and* OIL

Then I will send rain on your land in its season,
both autumn and spring rains, so that you may
gather in your grain, new wine, and olive oil.

DEUTERONOMY 11:14

THE BOUNTY OF THE LORD

If the promises were more important than the promised land, we should be very clear about what these promises were. The language of the passage above became a significant and recurring way in which God's promises were encapsulated.

In Deuteronomy 7, the promises are used to describe God's "covenant of love" with His people. "He will love you and bless you and increase your numbers. He will bless the fruit of your womb, the crops of your land—your grain, new wine, and olive oil—the calves of your herds and the lambs of your flocks." (Deuteronomy 7:13)

These blessings were intended to be a great source of joy for the children of Israel. "They will come and shout for joy on the heights of Zion; they will rejoice in the bounty of the

Lord—the grain, the new wine, and the olive oil, the young of the flocks and herds." (Jeremiah 31:12)

However, when Israel became fat and happy, she failed to recognize God as her source. "She has not acknowledged that I was the one who gave her the grain, the new wine and oil, who lavished on her the silver and gold—which they used for Baal." (Hosea 2:8) What God intended to be celebrated in Israel's feasts as "the bounty of the Lord" was perverted and lavished on other gods. In this way the covenant was broken and its blessings were revoked.

Even so, the blessings of the covenant were not lost on all the people. In an earlier time King David expressed his thanks for them in a beautiful way. "He makes grass grow for the cattle, and plants for people to cultivate—bringing forth food from the earth: wine that gladdens human hearts, oil to make their faces shine, and bread that sustains their hearts." (Psalm 104:14-15) Note that even though David substitutes bread for grain, neither the beauty nor the meaning of the phrase is lost.

*T*HE NEW COVENANT

Since our focus is on God's promises to us under the new covenant, it is important to see whether or not these elements of the promise carried over to the New Testament. In fact, not only are they present, but they have become even more significant.

Two of the elements are represented in the last supper—and the sacrament of communion—by the bread and wine. "The Lord Jesus, on the night he was betrayed, took bread, and when he had given thanks, he broke it and said, 'This is my body, which is for you; do this in remembrance of me.' In the same way, after supper he took the cup saying, 'This cup is the new covenant in my blood; do this whenever you drink it, in remembrance of me.' For whenever you eat this bread and drink this cup, you proclaim the Lord's death until he comes." (1 Corinthians 11:23-26)

In chapter 3 we saw that God wanted Pharaoh to let His people go so that they could hold a feast to Him in the desert. Then we observed that when the prodigal returned, the father was eager to kill the fattened calf and hold a feast in his honor. Jesus instituted another kind of feast in the form of the Lord's Supper, the shadow of which was the feast of the harvest described in Exodus 23:16. The feast of the harvest celebrated the grain, new wine, and oil. And let's not forget the parable of the feast recorded in Matthew 22 and Luke 14.

God likes feasts. He is always calling His people to a feast and not to a whipping. Whether they carry the stench of idolatry from Egypt or the smell of the prodigal's pigpen, as soon as His children turn to Him, He welcomes them with open arms. When it comes to His people, He is the God of acceptance, not of judgment. There is no reason to draw back from His presence.

Grain (Bread)

For most of us, bread is no big deal. It literally fills an entire aisle at the grocery store. White, wheat, rye, whole grain, seven grain, sliced, buns, rolls, French ... you name it and it is probably there. We usually think of bread as being mostly for sandwiches and optional for dinner.

In biblical times, this was not the case. Bread, especially for the poor, was life. It was the one thing they could not do without. Lacking bread, they were probably going to go hungry. No wonder David said it sustained the people's hearts.

Bread had not lost its significance in the time of Christ. It's no coincidence that it was one of the items Satan tried to use in the temptation of Jesus. But Jesus' response was to quote Deuteronomy 8:3b, "Man does not live on bread alone, but on every word that comes from the mouth of God."

Jesus, the Word who was with God in the beginning, declared that He was the bread of heaven in John 6, verses 33, 35, and 58. By partaking in communion we acknowledge His body, broken for us. The resurrected Christ is the living Word, and He still speaks. We need both the written word and His spoken word for our daily sustenance. We cannot expect to maintain a healthy spiritual life without the bread of God's word.

Jesus blessed a few pieces of bread, and those morsels fed more than 5,000 people. He wanted to show us there is no shortage of bread when we come to Him. His bread is most fresh and vital when we take it directly from His hand. We need not wait till Sunday for someone to feed us.

> Why spend money on what is not bread, and your labor on what does not satisfy? Listen, listen to me and eat what is good, and you will delight in the richest of fare." (Isaiah 55:2)

God understands that we need bread to sustain our hearts, and He wants our hearts to be sustained. Why is God so intent on our hearts? Because that's where the battle takes place. The price has already been paid for our forgiveness and salvation. That part of the war has already been won. But the real battle is for intimacy with God. That is the prize for which the Father paid such a great price. If Satan can get us to turn our hearts away from God, he wins.

"This is how we know what love is: Jesus Christ laid down his life for us." (1 John 3:16) Jesus did not die just to save us. He died to show us what love is. He died to bring us back to God. "This is how we know that we belong to the truth and how we set our hearts at rest in his presence: if our hearts condemn us, we know that God is greater than our hearts, and he knows everything." (1 John 3:19-20)

God wants to be our source. He wants to commune with us. He wants us to rest in His presence. Resting in His presence is the purest kind of worship.

God knows everything. He knows what our hearts looked like in the most evil moment of our lives, and He still decided to give His Son for us. He paid that price for us because He figured we were worth it. That is how badly He wants to connect with us.

New Wine

We are often told that the wine of communion represents the blood of Christ, shed for the forgiveness of our sins. While this is true, it is not the entire truth Christ communicated when He instituted the Lord's Supper. He stated, "This cup is the new covenant in my blood." (Luke 22:20) Jesus shed His blood and died not just to save us, but to bring us under the new covenant. If we look to His blood only for salvation, we despise our inheritance and miss out on many of the blessings He died to give us.

The new covenant promises of God are our promised land, our inheritance here on earth. Without them we are only occupying real estate. For our promises to be better, they have to be different from the old ones. Let's look at some of the differences.

+ *It's not about the law.* "I will put my law in their minds and write it on their hearts." (Jeremiah 31:33) This does not mean we will be able to memorize the law or even do better at applying it. Rather, we are under a completely different standard, which is the law of the Spirit. "Through Jesus Christ the law of the Spirit who gives life has set you free from the law of sin and death." (Romans 8:2) This means we have the ability to know how to please God in different situations as we allow Him to speak to our hearts through the Holy Spirit.

+ *Animal sacrifice is no longer necessary.* Since it was impossible for the blood of bulls and goats to take away sins, Christ became the lamb of God, sacrificed once and for all to make us holy. (Hebrews 10:1-8)

+ *The priests of the old covenant have been replaced by the Lord Jesus Christ.* (Hebrews 7:11-26) Jesus, our high priest forever, intercedes for us from His position at the right hand of God. Through him, "A better hope is introduced, by which we draw near to God." (Hebrews 7:19) By grace, we have been given the right to approach God just as freely as any pastor, preacher, or priest.

+ *God's kingdom has been established on earth, and only those who have been born of the Spirit may enter the kingdom.* (John 3:5) A kingdom is any realm in which the will of the king is obeyed. God's kingdom comes to earth inasmuch as His will is done here, thus Jesus' prayer in Matthew 6:10. We advance the kingdom of God when we bring His authority to bear on the situations we face in life and promote His will being done in those situations.

+ *They will all know me.* "'No longer will they teach their neighbor, or say to one another, "Know the Lord," because they will all know me, from the least of them to the greatest,' declares the Lord." (Jeremiah 31:34)

The new covenant is so much more than just the promise of heaven. It is a new way of relating to God whereby we are invited to come into His presence, hear His voice, and walk in relationship with Him. Again, He wants communion with us.

The purpose of new wine is to make our hearts glad. God never intended for "happy Christian" to be an oxymoron. There is incredible joy in walking in fellowship with God, obeying His leading, and stepping out into the next adventure He has for us.

How much new wine do you want? How much do you dare ask for? Jesus' very first miracle was to turn water into wine. By the way, this happened at a wedding feast, one of those things God seems to like. Do you remember what Jesus asked for? Jars. He is looking for vessels. He wants to fill us so full that we spill out God's goodness onto others.

Here is the problem with our jars. They are too full of *us* for the wine of the new covenant to squeeze into.

Oil

Most scholars agree that five symbols are used in scripture to represent the Holy Spirit: a dove, water, wind (or breath), fire, and oil. If oil is the third element of the bounty of the Lord, the Holy Spirit is the third part of our inheritance.

In biblical times, people used olive oil for preparing food. In addition, people put it on their faces to make them shine, the exact opposite of what most people desire for their faces today.

A third use of oil was in lamps where it was burned to provide light. That would have made it as important to the Israelites as electricity is to us.

Another use of oil is revealed in the story of the Good Samaritan, who poured oil into the man's wounds to promote healing.

And finally, oil was used for anointing.

*T*HE OIL OF ANOINTING

"Then Moses took the anointing oil and anointed the tabernacle and everything in it, and so consecrated them. He sprinkled some of the oil on the altar seven times, anointing it and all its utensils and the basin with its stand, to consecrate them. He poured some of the anointing oil on Aaron's head and anointed him to consecrate him." (Leviticus 8:10)

Anointing oil was used to consecrate, or set apart, someone or something for special use. First applied to the tabernacle and the priests, it was later also used to show that someone had been chosen for the office of prophet or king. The anointing oil came to represent the blessing, protection, and empowerment of God on the life of an individual.

At Jesus' baptism the Holy Spirit descended on Him, signifying that He is our prophet, priest, and king. A voice from heaven declared, "This is my Son, whom I love; with him I am well pleased." (Matthew 3:16-17)

This marked the beginning of Christ's ministry. The Holy Spirit was the anointing that made Jesus the Christ and Messiah (both of these words mean "anointed one"). Peter spoke to those in the household of Cornelius about "how God anointed Jesus of Nazareth with the Holy Spirit and power, and how he went around doing good and healing all who were under the power of the devil, because God was with him." (Acts 10:38)

We can clearly see the power of this anointing by observing the Spirit's impact on the life of Jesus from His baptism forward:

+ "Jesus, full of the Holy Spirit, left the Jordan and was led by the Spirit into the wilderness, where for 40 days he was tempted by the devil." (Luke 4:1-2)

+ "Jesus returned to Galilee in the power of the Spirit, and the news about him spread throughout the whole countryside." (Luke 4:14)

+ "He went to Nazareth, where he had been brought up, and on the Sabbath day he went into the synagogue, as was his custom. He stood up to read, and the scroll of the prophet Isaiah was handed to him. Unrolling it, he found the place where it is written: 'The Spirit of the Lord is on me, because he has anointed me to proclaim good news to the poor. He has sent me to proclaim freedom for the prisoners and recovery of sight for the blind, to set the oppressed free, to proclaim the year of the Lord's favor." (Luke 4-17-19)

This happened in Nazareth, Jesus' home town. He had gone into the synagogue there many times—it was His custom to do so. The people had heard Him read from the scrolls before, and it appears He had never previously made any unusual claims. But on this particular day, after receiving the baptism of the Holy Spirit, He claimed, "The Lord has anointed me.... Today this scripture is fulfilled in your hearing." (Luke 4:21)

*H*OW DID HE DO IT?

I used to believe Jesus had the power to do miraculous things because He was the Son of God. But according to the book of Philippians, "Though he was God, he did not think of equality with God as something to cling to. Instead, he *gave up his divine privileges*; he took the humble position of a slave and was born as a human being" (Philippians 2:6-7, NLT). Other versions say He "made himself nothing" (NIV) or "emptied himself" (NASB and NET).

Rather than getting lost in a deep theological discussion of exactly which interpretation is right or exactly what the words mean, let's back up and come at it from a different angle. How did Jesus do the things He did?

How did Jesus drive out demons? He told the Pharisees, "But if it is by the Spirit of God that I drive out demons, then the kingdom of God has come upon you." (Mathew 12:28)

How did Jesus heal? "One day Jesus was teaching, and the Pharisees and teachers of the law were sitting there…and the power of the Lord was with Jesus to heal the sick." (Luke 5:17)

How did Jesus speak to the disciples? "In my former book, Theophilus, I wrote about all that Jesus began to do and to teach until the day he was taken up to heaven, after giving instructions through the Holy Spirit to the apostles he had chosen." (Acts 1:1-2)

How did Jesus live a perfect life? The book of Hebrews speaks of the sanctifying power of the blood of Christ, "who through the eternal Spirit offered himself unblemished to God." (Hebrews 9:14)

What if Jesus did everything He did on earth by the power of the Holy Spirit?

If Jesus emptied himself of everything that came with being the Son of God and was subsequently filled with the Holy Spirit who anointed Him and empowered Him to do the things He did, it would explain a whole lot. In the first place, it would agree with the spirit of all the scriptures we have just examined. It is also the only way to explain the one statement Jesus made that we all seem to have so much trouble with. "Very truly I tell you, whoever believes in me will do the works I have been doing, and they will do even greater things than these, because I am going to the Father." (John 14:12)

THEY WERE CALLED CHRISTIANS

If the same Spirit who lived in Christ Jesus lived in us, we could do what Jesus did. There would be no mystery and no explaining away what Jesus said. The Bible would be as real and relevant to us today as it was to those who spent time with the Lord and then did the same kinds of things He did after He ascended to heaven. God's Kingdom could be on earth as it is in heaven, and His people could get on with being His people and acting in accordance with His nature.

All these things that seem so incredible to us are simply the way God intended for things to be.

What were the people who walked in the Way of Jesus called? They were called Christians. Anointed ones. If they had only tried to go to church and be good, rational, and nicey-nicey they simply could have been called Jesusians or The Saved. They would have lived just like we do, and the Bible could have ended with the book of John.

"But you have an anointing from the Holy One." (1 John 2:20)

That's why the story didn't end. That's why there was still plenty to see, to hear, and to tell about. And if that same anointing is not available to us, then we are not living under the new covenant.

*B*ETTER PROMISES

As has already been stated, the Holy Spirit is the central promise of the new covenant. "I will pour out my Spirit on all people. Your sons and daughters will prophesy, your old men will dream dreams, and your young men will see visions. Even on my servants, both men and women, I will pour out my Spirit in those days." (Joel 2:28-29)

The promise of the Holy Spirit goes all the way back to Abraham in the book of Genesis. "He redeemed us in order that the blessing given to Abraham might come to the Gentiles through Jesus Christ, so that we might receive the promise of the Spirit…. For if the inheritance depends on the law, then it no longer depends on a promise; but God in his grace gave it to Abraham through a promise." (Galatians 3:14,18)

On the day of Pentecost Peter told the astonished crowd of people, "God has raised this Jesus to life, and we are all witnesses of it. Exalted to the right hand of God, he has received from the Father the promised Holy Spirit and has poured out what you now see and hear." (Acts 2:33)

The gift of the Holy Spirit has been given. The anointing oil has been poured out on God's people. The new covenant is in place and will continue unchanged until the return of Jesus. The anointing, blessing, protection, and power of the Holy Spirit should be evident in everything we do. Because of the Spirit there is still much to see, hear, and testify to even in our generation.

"The Spirit speaks to us. What he speaks to us about is our identity as God's children and the inheritance that goes with that…whose we are and what belongs to us."[1] And what belongs to us is almost beyond comprehension.

* ✶ *

1 Alan Smith, *Unveiled,* p. 59.

POWER

CHAPTER 12

ALEXANDER THE MEDIOCRE

I pray also... that you may know...
his incomparably great power for us who believe.

EPHESIANS 1:18

WHAT MAKES A KING GREAT?

Alexander the Great was just Alexander until he conquered most of the known world. His ambition drove him to use his resources to conquer more and more nations. To say it another way, he used his power to expand his kingdom. The extent of his success caused him to be recognized as great. His kingdom brought him glory.

The same can be said of King Solomon. He was not only renowned for his wisdom, his kingdom was the greatest in the history of Israel. He conquered so many kings and acquired so much wealth that he made silver as common as stones in Jerusalem. (2 Chronicles 9:27)

Jesus closed the Lord's Prayer by saying, "For Yours is the kingdom and the power and the glory forever. Amen." (Matthew 6:13) Kingdom, power, and glory go together.

What does God want His kingdom to say about Him? Is God reserving all His glory for heaven when the streets will be paved with gold? If so, Jesus should have said, "For Yours will be the kingdom, the power, and the glory forever."

As we keep finding out regarding the things of God, His kingdom is both a now and a later kingdom. Jesus often taught the people that the kingdom was near or that it was upon them. (Matthew 12:28) He also taught that we should pray for the kingdom to come. (Matthew 6:10)

So, like our inheritance, the kingdom has a now glory and a later (and greater) glory. The questions we should be asking are, "Would He want a wimpy kingdom today that brought Him no glory?" and "What kind of contribution is the church supposed to make toward His kingdom on earth?"

In our time it has become popular for businesses and even churches to have a vision statement, a purpose statement, or some combination of the two. Leadership can then look at organizational practices to see whether or not they are moving the organization toward its goals.

God must have thought this was a good idea because He has a purpose statement for the church. This statement uses language that is nothing short of incomprehensible to anyone who is not comfortable with the workings of the Holy Spirit. That is probably why it has mostly been ignored.

> His intent was that now, through the church, the manifold wisdom of God should be made known to the rulers and authorities in the heavenly realms, according to his eternal purpose that he accomplished in Christ Jesus our Lord. (Ephesians 3:10-11)

Hmmm. God's intent is to reveal His manifold wisdom through the church. That is His plan and purpose for us.

Appropriately, Paul follows this passage with a prayer. It seems he knew what they were up against and had some idea how difficult it might be to display the manifold wisdom of God. Here are the things he prays for:

+ That they be strengthened with power through His Spirit in their inner being.
+ That Christ might dwell in their hearts through faith.
+ That they be rooted and established in love.
+ That they grasp the full extent of the love of Christ.
+ That they be filled to the measure of all the fullness of God.

Okay, God. Giving us those five things sounds like a step in the right direction. These things might be possible to apprehend if you really and fully fill us with your Spirit. Anything else?

Glory In the Church

"Now to him who is able to do immeasurably more than all we ask or imagine, according to his power that is at work within us, to him be glory in the church and in Christ Jesus throughout all generations, for ever and ever! Amen." (Ephesians 3:20-21)

God wants to receive glory in the church. It started in Acts and was supposed to continue through all generations and then on into eternity.

But the unthinkable has happened. We have adopted a *form* of godliness while denying its power. Terrible times are upon us. (2 Timothy 3:1)

What happened? Someone unplugged the cord and said, "Enough of this power. Enough of this Holy Spirit. It's more comfortable without Him." The Bible commands us to have nothing to do with people who think and act like that. (2 Timothy 3:5) I'm afraid that would keep us out of a lot of churches these days.

Glory refers to the value of something. It has to do with weight. For example, a nugget of gold is worth a certain amount of money based on its weight.

We live in a weightless society, obsessed with things that will make no difference in eternity. It seems we spend a lot of our time, energy, and money on things that do not matter. We need enough glory to keep us from blowing away.[1]

To separate the kingdom from the power means God gets no glory.

It leaves the church stuck in the middle of nowhere and irrelevant to the problems of the world. It's spiritual suicide—death by indifference.

God, our proud Father, wants His children to do well. He has promised us His incomparably great power for those who believe. Incomparably great power for what—being good?

The only reason we would need great power is if God wanted us to do the things Jesus did. He never, never wanted to deny us the gift of the Holy Spirit. The Bible specifically says so. "If you then, though you are evil, know how to give good gifts to your children, how much more will your Father in heaven give the Holy Spirit to those who ask him?" (Luke 11:13)

Jesus said the miracles He did were evidence that the kingdom of God was near. (Matthew 12:28) Now that He has ascended, His kingdom has been established on earth. (Colossians 1:13) How can the before be better than the after? It can't.

---

1   Craig Terndrup, *Praise—The Starting Point,* Gateway Church, March 3, 2008.

Do Not Seek and You Will Not Find

People naturally seek comfort. We want comfortable clothes, cars, and homes. We even go for comfort foods. But too much comfort is not good for us. If life was supposed to be comfortable, we would not need the Comforter.

Through the apostle John, Jesus told the church at Laodicea, "You say, 'I am rich; I have acquired wealth and do not need a thing.' But you do not realize that you are wretched, pitiful, poor, blind, and naked." (Revelation 3:17)

A church that needs nothing stops seeking. If all we need is salvation, then *we do not need God now*. And if we are not seeking God, we are very likely not going to find Him!

Wherever there is access to power lines, there are warning signs. Power is dangerous. Unfortunately, the church has settled for life without power because life without power seems comfortable, safe, and under control. But it also leaves us wretched, pitiful, poor, blind, and naked. Pitiful, power-less churches will never bring God the glory He wants and deserves.

Knowledge

Most church services I have attended are what I would call "sermon based." There is a brief time of "worship," which often consists of a few songs and a prayer. Then follows the sermon, usually presented by the pastor who has at least been to seminary and may very well have a Ph.D. In most cases, the sermon is the main dish and may take up the lion's share of the service time.

This traditional structure for the service would seem to indicate that knowledge is the most important aspect of Christianity. The pastor gets paid to study the Bible and preach the sermons. He knows more than we do, and it is his job to impart knowledge to us to help us serve God better.

Can you remember the subject of last Sunday's sermon? Did it materially help you serve God better on Monday or for the rest of the week? Maybe the sermon is not the most important thing that is supposed to happen on Sunday.

Do you "go to church" or do you go to stand united with your brothers and sisters in God's presence and worship Him for His incredible love, mercy, goodness, and grace?

It seems like somewhere along the line we may have forgotten that the object of our worship is God. We were created to serve the Father, Son, and Holy Spirit, not the Father, Son and Holy Bible.

Let me clearly state that I am in no way attempting to diminish the importance of Scripture. The Bible is the inspired word of God. It stands as the final word on truth and doctrine. We should feed on it daily, and it is the primary means through which we should hear the voice of God. But it is not our source of life. God is.

I fear that sermon-based church has taught us to listen, learn, feel better, and do nothing. Study...won't heal the brokenhearted or set the captives free. We come; we learn; we leave. It is not enough.[2]

*P*OWER

Knowledge does not have the power to change us. Only God can do that.

If God is strong, does He want weak sons? We have been so deceived that we think strong men play football. No. Strong

---

2   Eldredge, *Waking the Dead*, p.194.

men take the kingdom by force. Strong men pray and travail for their family's spiritual well-being. Strong men put on the armor of God and fight for the kingdom of God with the sword of the Spirit.

We do not need more knowledge as much as we need more of God. God wants us to have the truth, not just knowledge. The truth is a person—Jesus Christ. Jesus is the way, the truth, and the life. He does not live in our heads; He indwells us in the form of the Spirit of truth, the counselor whom Jesus promised would be with us forever. (John 14:16-18)

Jesus' miracles were evidence of the kingdom. He is supernatural and will do the supernatural in us and through us if we only believe. He is our strength. We must press into our strength, not fear Him.

The apostle Paul was very clear about this:

+ "My message and my preaching were not with wise and persuasive words, but with a demonstration of the Spirit's power, so that your faith might rest not on men's wisdom, but on God's power." (1 Corinthians 2:4)

+ "For we know brothers and sisters loved by God, that he has chosen you, because our gospel came to you not simply with words, but also with power, with the Holy Spirit and deep conviction." (1 Thessalonians 1:4-5)

+ "For the kingdom of God is not a matter of talk, but of power." (1 Corinthians 4:20)

There should be no difference between the church today and the church we read about in the New Testament. We live under the same covenant—the one that really is better. That covenant is sealed by the blood of Jesus and can never change.

Finding His Heart

We have not believed because we have not understood the Father. When we find Him, we come to know His heart. And when we find God's heart, we find our own. Only in Him can we find our purpose, and our purpose unlocks our passion.

We must step out in faith to see the power of God in our generation. It starts with prayer. But prayer has meaning only if we actually think God might do something. Prayer brings God into the present moment. It puts us in a position to see things from His perspective. It puts us in the middle of somewhere.

Spiritual seeing and hearing are not about the situation in front of us, but about what God wants to do in that situation. Our availability allows God to be a change agent through us.

How Much Is It Worth?

Israel had to fight for its inheritance, the promised land. The Bible tells us our glorious inheritance is "in the saints." (Ephesians 1:18) Our inheritance on earth is in the people who make up the church, the kingdom that is supposed to bring Him glory.

The church is our promise land, the place in which we were meant to receive the blessings of the new covenant. Something amazing is supposed to happen there as we function as the body of Christ. God expects us to reach unity in the faith and to grow to such a level of maturity that we attain the whole measure of the fullness of Christ. (Ephesians 4:13) I don't know about you, but I can see that bringing God some glory. Would that be worth fighting for?

TREASURE IN OUR HEARTS

There is treasure in our promise land. The treasure is in our hearts. It is the light of the knowledge of God's glory in the face of Christ. (2 Corinthians 4:6) It is enlightenment of the heart which reveals the hope to which we are called. (Ephesians 1:18) Our hope is to bring glory to God by representing the fullness of Christ to heaven and earth.

God in His great wisdom knew that even when filled with the Holy Spirit, no single one of us could fully represent Christ on earth. So He put us together in the church to be His body. In a beautiful synergy, the body is built up as each part does its work. (Ephesians 4:16) This mutual building up is supposed to bring us to such a place of maturity that when someone looks at us as a whole, we look just like Jesus.

This can happen only in a divine/human partnership. "God supplies the wisdom, direction and power. We supply the body and voice. His is the kingdom, power, and glory. Ours is the asking. We can't do it without Him. He won't do it without us."[3]

Not even our pastors can represent Jesus by themselves. Many pastors may burn out trying, but it will never happen. Nor is it the pastor's job to do the work of the church. It is the pastor's job to help the people in the church get equipped to do the work of the church. And he cannot even do this job by himself.

"So Christ himself gave the apostles, the prophets, the evangelists, the pastors and teachers, to equip his people for works of service, so that the body of Christ may be built up

---

3   Sheets, *Watchman Prayer*, p. 57.

until we all reach unity in the faith and in the knowledge of the Son of God and become mature, attaining the whole measure of the fullness of Christ." (Ephesians 4:11-13)

Churches that have explained away apostles and prophets have explained away 40 percent of the equipping of the saints. And the pastors who preach the very best sermons week after week can get only 20 percent of the job done, at best. "God deliver us from being in a church where most of the congregation don't feel any sense of responsibility for the work. If we don't [act] collectively for the church, it means we are missing out on the heart of God for the community."[4]

If we believed in our inheritance—in God's promises—we would act differently. We would accept the Holy Spirit with open arms, recognizing Him as the Spirit of wisdom and revelation without whom we can neither know God nor represent Him on earth. We would see Him as the glue and nails by which the church is built up and without which it cannot stand.

If we believed in our inheritance, "God said" would become the most important words in existence and what man has said would cease to leave the church without power and direction, and without the hope Christ died to give us. We would know who we are because we know who God is, and the supernatural would be as real to us as anything we can touch or see.

✳ ✳ ✳

---

4 Cooke, *Developing Your Prophetic Gifting*, p. 69.

CHAPTER 13

THE FULLNESS *of* CHRIST

Blessed are those who hunger and thirst
for righteousness, for they will be filled.

MATTHEW 5:6

TRUE VERSUS TRUTH

The Bible is more than true; it is truth. Things that are true are often put into writing and filed away. They disappear into the realm of interesting facts that can be stored somewhere and looked up when needed.

Truth is different. When truth is properly applied, life changes. Truth is not really truth until it is put into action.

For example, a bullet can be put into a rifle and used to shoot game that can be eaten to sustain life. This is an indisputable fact. It's true. But when the game is shot and eaten, the hunter has changed it into something real and actual. If I eat some of the meat, the truth of the statement comes to realization for me. The facts have been brought to life.

I know there is such a place as Bombay, India. I can look it up, see pictures, and read about it. There are many facts about Bombay that I could learn. No doubt, many of them would be very interesting. But I have never experienced Bombay because I have never been there.

I also know there is a place called Austin, Texas. I should. I live there. I experience Austin every day. It cannot be separated from the things I do because I am in the midst of it. Its people, sights, sounds, and tastes are woven into the fabric of my life. Austin is more than a fact to me. It is part of who I am.

*Y*OUR WORD IS TRUTH

We have come to treat the Bible like it is true, but not truth. This has wreaked desolation on our spiritual lives. Consider the scripture quoted above. "Blessed are those who hunger and thirst for righteousness, for they will be filled." From the lives of a lot of Christians I have observed over my lifetime, it is pretty clear that many have failed to grasp the clear and simple truth of it. There has been a disconnect between the words, which we would all affirm as true, and the lives we are living. We mostly seem to be running half empty.

The words are so simple. "Blessed" is easy enough. It means happy. Abundant.

"Hunger and thirst." Most of us should get that. It means going after something as if your life depended upon it. Seeking something with passion.

But what does "righteousness" look like?

Exactly how are we to be filled?

*R*IGHTEOUSNESS

Satan has made us afraid of righteousness. In this the gain is all his, the loss all ours.

Righteousness means right relationship with God. There is nothing to fear about relating to God. He is the kindest, most loving being in existence. But as crazy as it may sound, Satan has convinced us to be afraid of being close to God.

We have everything to lose in that. We lose knowing God. No wonder we live lives so full of hurt and loneliness.

Satan uses any of several effective arguments. "God only wants to shame us by exposing our sin. It's too hard. It's not fun. It'll wait."

God doesn't need to expose our sin. It's already exposed. We are naked before him, and we will feel ashamed as long as we continue to walk in sin. He doesn't want us to feel ashamed. He wants to set us free, not judge us.

The father did not shame his prodigal son. He asked for no list of wrongs committed and repented of. He ran to him and embraced him. He gave him a new robe and let him start over, clean.

God wants to set us free to worship and to fellowship with Him. He wants to father us and have us feast at His table.

It's not hard for us to please God; it's impossible. Performance will always kill us, so God took performance out of the picture. He gave us the righteousness of His Son. It's a free gift. All we need to do is believe and receive.

Righteousness is fun. God wants our best. Sin always damages the sinner. God wants to protect us from that. His boundaries are for our safety, not so that He can visit His righteous indignation upon us when we cross the line.

God created us for a reason, and we will feel fulfilled and happy only when we are actively living out His purpose in our lives. Nothing else can satisfy us.

After the father received the prodigal son home, he threw a celebration. The feast God is calling us to is better than a party. The difference is that at His feast, God gets the glory. At a party someone or something else does.

At a party we are just passing time and looking for substitutes. "Eat, drink, and be merry, for tomorrow we die."

With God we are doing what we were created to do. We are moving toward our destinies. We are filled and fulfilled. Life becomes a continual feast. (Proverbs 15:15) And tomorrow we live.

It can't wait. In the parable of the 10 virgins, Jesus warned us to always be ready for His return. The difference between the five wise and the five foolish virgins is that the foolish virgins had no oil for their lamps.

The difference between those who are ready for the return of Jesus and those who are not is the oil of the Holy Spirit. Without the ongoing work of the Holy Spirit the New Testament becomes the new law, not the new covenant. In that case, Christ need not have died, because any law is sufficient to kill us.

Those with no oil cannot enter the feast, because there is no relationship—no "Spirit of sonship." (Romans 8:15) The bridegroom's response to the virgins who have no oil is, "I don't know you." (Matthew 25:12) This is yet another affirmation that righteousness means right relationship.

$\mathcal{T}$HEY SHALL BE FILLED

We ought to know what it means to be filled. We need to know with what (or, more correctly, with whom) we can be filled. We have to know how full we should be.

We have to find fullness. It's God's plan for the church. "So that the body of Christ may be built up until we all reach unity in the faith and in the knowledge of the Son of God and become mature, attaining to the whole measure of the fullness of Christ." (Ephesians 4:12-13)

Remember that we are talking about filling a hunger and thirst. Jesus made other references to this matter. One was to the Samaritan woman He visited with at the well of Sychar. He asked her for a drink and she responded somewhat defensively:

> How can you ask me for a drink?
>
> Jesus answered her, "If you knew the gift of God and who it is that asks you for a drink, you would have asked him and he would have given you living water....
>
> "Everyone who drinks this water will be thirsty again, but whoever drinks the water I give them will never thirst. Indeed, the water I give them will become a spring of water welling up to eternal life." (John 4:9-10, 13-14)

This is the water we need to thirst for — the water that satisfies and wells up to eternal life. Jesus picked up this theme later at the Feast of Tabernacles.

> "Let anyone who is thirsty come to me and drink. Whoever believes in me, as the Scripture has said, rivers of living water will flow from them." By this he meant the Spirit, whom those who believed in him were later to receive. Up to that time the Spirit had not been given, since Jesus had not yet been glorified." (John 7:37-39)

Only the Holy Spirit can fill us. When He does, we get so full that we overflow onto others. We have so much life in us that others want it. Imagine a church where every member displayed this fullness. That is what God planned for us — the fullness of Christ.

What You Do Know Can Hurt You

If you asked Christians today why Jesus came to earth, I believe the vast majority would say, "To provide forgiveness for my sins and make a way for me to go to heaven." This is very true, but it is an incomplete answer. The wholesale acceptance of this truth as being all we need to know may be cutting us off from all we need to learn.

As with every other person He has ever placed upon this planet, God had a design for Jesus' life. As the only perfect human, Jesus understood His purpose and, without a doubt, stands as the only individual who ever accomplished everything He was sent to do.

Jesus came here and lived as one of us. He came in obedience to the Father. He did it because it was the Father's plan. If we are unsure just what that plan was, perhaps we should find out.

Angels announced the birth of Jesus and declared to the shepherds God's reason for sending Him. "Today in the town of David a Savior has been born to you; he is the Messiah, the Lord." (Luke 2:11)

*N*EWS FLASH

Angels are good messengers. They get straight to the point, and they say what God tells them to say without a lot of frills or interpretation. Here is a very loose representation of their message to the shepherds that night.

"Good evening from the Angelic News Network. We now interrupt this night of watching sheep for a breaking story. Something big is happening."

"When?"

"Today."

"Where?"

"In the town of David."

"What?"

"The birth of a child."

"Why?"

"To be your Savior. To be the Messiah. To be your Lord."

Here is the sobering thought for the day. Those who think Jesus came to save us are 33 percent correct. That would get you an "F" in just about any class, anywhere.

Many times, the most difficult things for us to learn are the things we think we already know. The Pharisees were so certain they knew the Scriptures and the proper interpretation of the Law that they were unable to make room in their thinking for Jesus, the incarnate Word of God and the Messiah for whom they were supposed to be looking. The truth of which they were so proud cut them off from the Truth who stood before them. (John 5:37-40)

We know Jesus came to save us. But it was never meant to stop there.

Who He Was

First, Jesus came to be the person God created Him to be. He was:

+ The Savior, the Lamb of God who sacrificed himself for us. (John 1:29)

+ The Messiah (the Christ), the one sent from God and anointed with the Holy Spirit. (Acts 2:36)

+ The Lord, the one whose presence demands a decision to obey or not to obey. (Romans 10:9)

Why He Came

Jesus came to accomplish what God wanted Him to accomplish. Jesus marked the beginning of His ministry by reading from the book of Isaiah. "The Spirit of the Lord is on me, because the Lord has anointed me to proclaim good news to the poor. He has sent me to proclaim freedom for the prisoners and recovery of sight for the blind, to set the oppressed free, to proclaim the year of the Lord's favor.... Today this scripture is fulfilled in your hearing." (Luke 4:18-21)

As His ministry progressed, Jesus made several other statements of purpose. He came:

+ To call sinners to repentance (Matthew 9:13)

+ To show us the Father (John 14:7)

+ To do God's will (John 6:38)

+ That we might have life (John 10:10)

+ As the light (John 12:46)

+ To give us the Holy Spirit (John 20:22)

We are not called only to repentance and salvation; we are called to be like Him. In fact, we are supposed to be so much like Him that when we properly function as His body, we attain to His fullness. To do so, we would have to be able to do what Jesus did ... share the good news with the poor, bring freedom for the prisoners and recovery of sight for the blind, release the oppressed, proclaim the year of the Lord's favor.

When we do these things, we are worshipping and pleasing God. "Through Jesus, therefore, let us continually offer to God a sacrifice of praise—the fruit of lips that openly profess his name. And do not forget to do good and share with others, for with such sacrifices God is pleased." (Hebrews 13:15-16)

Robert Morris says worship is love expressed. We worship God when we act like Jesus. As He sacrificed, we must also sacrifice. This primarily means ministering to and blessing people.

MANIFESTATIONS OF THE SPIRIT

If we try to act like Jesus in our own power, we only become good actors. It takes His power working through us for us to be like Him. "Now may the God of peace … equip you with everything good for doing his will, and may he work in us what is pleasing to him, through Jesus Christ, to whom be glory forever and ever. Amen." (Hebrews 13:20-21)

It would be unfair for God to expect us to act like Jesus while refusing to equip us for the task. We must do what we do through Jesus as He empowers us by the Holy Spirit. (Luke 24:49)

The entire reason for the existence of the church is so that it can grow up to be the body of Christ and to represent Him in all His fullness to the world. As a part of one body, each of us, by grace, has been given something to contribute to the church. Some of the gifts we can and should expect to be expressed are listed in 1 Corinthians:

> Now to each one the manifestation of the Spirit is given for the common good. To one there is given through the Spirit a message of wisdom, to another a message of knowledge by means of the same Spirit, to another faith by the same Spirit, to another gifts of healing by that one Spirit, to another miraculous powers, to another prophecy, to another distinguishing between spirits, to another speaking in different kinds of tongues, and to still another the interpretation of tongues. All these are the work of one and the same Spirit, and he distributes them to each one, just as he determines. (1 Corinthians 12:7-11)

This should completely revolutionize the way we look at our brothers and sisters. From a human perspective we tend to see their weaknesses and limitations. We look at their physical appearance, natural abilities, social standing, and status. Only God can open our eyes to see them as His temple, the place where God dwells, the place where heaven and earth meet, and the place where God's glory rests.[1]

We must see each other as God's gifts to one another, filled with the Holy Spirit and equipped to build us up into the glorious house of God. We can't do it alone. The Spirit alone will do it though us.

That is the only kind of church that can represent the fullness of Christ. We could expect these gifts to be absent only if Jesus came to give us minimum life, just barely enough life, or life in survival mode. Instead, He came to give us abundant life, fullness of life, eternal life that starts now and expands into eternity. Why would we want to settle for anything less?

* + *

---

1   Smith, *Unveiled,* p. 138.

CHAPTER 14

WHERE THERE'S A WAY, THERE'S A WILL

There is a way that appears to be right.
but in the end it leads to death.

PROVERBS 14:12

$\mathcal{J}$ saw a billboard the other day declaring, "Jesus is the Answer." That would apply to the model of the needs-oriented church in which God is expected to fix all problems and answer all questions. If Jesus is Mr. Fix It, we are in charge. Thanks be to God, Jesus is much more than that.

Jesus never said He was the answer. His claim was much more informative, "I am the way and the truth and the life. No one comes to the Father except through me." (John 14:6) Jesus is the way to the Father, not the answer to all our concerns.

I have already written quite a bit about Jesus as the truth and the life. Now let's look at Jesus as the way.

*M*AKING A WAY

If we wanted to make a way between two towns or cities, there would be a lot of things to take into consideration. First, we would need to acquire the land for it. We would do this by purchasing the right of way.

Ways need to last a long time, so they should be built of materials that will endure, such as rock, concrete, or asphalt. Water causes much damage to ways, so ours needs to be elevated—a high way—so that water will drain off. "Low ways" are not the way to go. Low ways often tend to look a lot like canals.

Since highways usually run through farms or ranches, good fences are necessary for keeping farm and ranch things on one side and travelers on the other. These fences usually have signs every so often on the highway side that say "No trespassing."

Additional informational signage would be needed to indicate distance to towns, speed limits, and rest stops. A good system for lighting our highway would also need to be considered.

*T*HE WRONG WAY TO USE THE RIGHT OF WAY

After Adam and Eve sinned, mankind needed a way to get back to the Father. The Law of Moses did not turn out to be the way. It was more like the fence on either side of the right of way. If men could stay between the fences and keep from trespassing, that meant they were on the right way. But that didn't mean they were making the right use of it. Close to the fence there are obstacles like mud, culverts, tumbleweeds, and all kinds of other things that slow down one's progress. That's not where we need to be if we want to make good time. What we need is to get on down the road.

The other problem with fences is that the stuff on the other side can be very appealing. We tend to keep looking for excuses to go over there. Maybe we want to look at something attractive or even take something that isn't ours. Maybe we just want to sit on the green grass and rest. Next thing you know, we forget we are even on a journey. Then we want to buy land and build a house.

Thus, the fences that were supposed to help became part of the problem:

  * "We ... know that a person is not justified by the works of the law." (Galatians 2:15-16)

  * "I found that the very commandment that was intended to bring life actually brought death. For sin, seizing the opportunity afforded by the commandment ... put me to death." (Romans 7:10-11)

  * "Therefore no one will be declared righteous in God's sight by the works of the law; rather, through the law we become conscious of our sin." (Romans 3:20)

We need to get off the wayside and onto the road. We don't have to live a sin-conscious life. There is a better way.

Jesus Is the Way

The Pharisees couldn't recognize Jesus, the Way, because they had made it all about the fence (the law). They watched the fence, looked for ways to make it better, and kept a sharp eye out for anyone who might trespass. Yep, they would rather stone someone than have them break the law. The fence was their pride and joy. The gift had become more important than the Giver.

We still have people like that today. If it's not about God, it can be about almost anything—who has the best doctrine,

knows the most Scripture, or doesn't play cards. But all that
amounts to is building new and "better" fences. The trouble
is, if you have your face to the fence, you pretty much have
your back to the way. The fruit of all that rule-book stuff is
generally the same now as it was then: pride, condemnation,
judgment, and spiritual blindness.

Jesus pulled no punches in confronting the Pharisees'
stupidity, often using colorful language that may seem to us
a little unkind — snakes, whitewashed walls, children of the
devil — you get the drift. He said these things to the experts
in the law His father had given Moses.

Jesus came to give us a way to be made right with God
without having to keep the law. (Romans 3:21-22, Romans
6:14) It is the way of faith, grace, and the Spirit (Romans 3-8).

So if it's not about the fence, what is it about? It's not about
performance, doctrine, the law, the fence, or even salvation.
It's about coming to the Father.

Better doctrine can't move us toward God; we need to find
the Way. We can't just learn what is true about God; we have
to find the Truth. We don't need better rules for living; we
must find the Life.

We're lost with only a *form* of godliness. We need God.
Our highest goal should be to know Him better.

THE WAY OF THE FATHER

There should be a reason for the way we do things. It should
make spiritual sense. It should be God's way of doing things,
not our own idea of how things should be done.

Sometimes when I do something, I say, "This is the way my
father would do it." When you know someone, it is easy to
walk in his ways. The book of Proverbs contains the wisdom of

King Solomon. Next time you read it, notice how many times it uses words like "way," "path," "walk," "course," or "steps."

> My son, if you accept my words and store up my commands within you, turning your ear to wisdom and applying your heart to understanding—indeed if you call out for insight and cry aloud for understanding, and if you look for it as for silver and search for it as for hidden treasure, then you will understand the fear of the Lord and find the knowledge of God. For the Lord gives wisdom, and from his mouth come knowledge and understanding. He holds success in store for the upright, he is a shield to those whose walk is blameless, for he guards the course of the just and protects the way of his faithful ones. (Proverbs 2:1-8)

The New Testament is also full of such references:

+ Jesus said, "I am the way and the truth and the life. No one comes to the Father except through me." (John 14:5) He is the way to the Father.

+ Paul went to Damascus to persecute those who "belonged to the Way." (Acts 9:2) At that time, Christianity was called "the Way."

+ Jesus said, "Small is the gate and narrow the road that leads to life." (Matthew 7:14) A road, not a set of commandments, leads to life.

Christianity is a way, a road, a journey. It is life that comes from knowing God, hearing God, and being led by God, not from following law.

THE WAY MY FATHER WOULD DO IT

How can Jesus, a person, be a way? As He lived His life, every action communicated, "This is the way my Father would do it." That's how we are supposed to live. We can know the Father well enough to know His ways—well enough to know how He would do it.

When my daughters were young, they would sometimes put on a skirt or dress and ask me if it was too short. As children, they probably needed this kind of direction. But for a mature Christian, this is the wrong question completely. The real question being asked in this example is, "How close can I walk to the fence and still get away with it?" It is the kind of question that can break a father's heart.

Let's look at another promise of the new covenant. "Your ears will hear a voice behind you saying, this is the way, walk in it." (Isaiah 30:21) This is yet another assurance of the gift of the Holy Spirit. "But if you are led by the Spirit, you are not under the law." (Galatians 5:18) He leads us in the way, not the law.

When we choose the way, we are set free to live conscious of God, not conscious of the law. When we are walking fully in the way, our faces are pointed toward God. When we are led by the Spirit, fences are completely unnecessary. The law is extraneous. We no longer need rules.

A LAMP FOR MY FEET

I mentioned earlier that our highway would need a good lighting system. That is one of the most beautiful functions of the Word of God. "Your word is a lamp for my feet, a light on my path." (Psalm 119:105) While the Bible is not, in and of itself, the way, it is God's wonderful lighting system for the way. But, of course, it is much more than that.

When we take in the Bible as our daily bread, it becomes part of us. It goes from being an external lighting system to being part of an internal guidance system. (Psalm 119:11). It takes up residence in our hearts and helps to sensitize us to the voice of the Holy Spirit. When the voice of the Bible and the voice of the Holy Spirit align, we are on target. We can walk in peace.

Furthermore, the Bible, as part of the *rhema* word of God, becomes our sword, "the sword of the Spirit." (Ephesians 6:17) Armed with it, we are prepared to face whatever crosses our way.

To Walk as Jesus Walked

"Whoever claims to live in him must walk as Jesus did." (1 John 2:6, NIV) Jesus walked in power. If we cannot walk in power, we cannot walk as Jesus walked. God would be asking us to do the impossible.

This reminds me of a story in Exodus. Moses and Aaron went to Pharaoh and told him to let the people of Israel go. Pharaoh did not exactly jump at this opportunity. Instead, he decided the slaves had too much time on their hands. They needed more work so they would have less time to think. He told the Egyptian foremen to stop supplying straw for the slaves, but not to reduce their quota of bricks. (Exodus 5:7-8)

This was a vengeful and oppressive action on the part of Pharaoh and everyone knew it. When the Israelite foremen found Moses and Aaron, they said, "May the Lord look on you and judge you! You have made us obnoxious to Pharaoh and his officials and have put a sword in their hand to kill us." (Exodus 5:20-21)

God is not like Pharaoh. He would never give us a mission without giving us the tools to perform it. It was and is and always will be God's heart to bless His people, not to bring difficulty down on their heads.

It is God's purpose to bring all things together in Christ and to advance His kingdom on earth. His desire is for us to achieve the fullness of Christ *in the church.* (Ephesians 4:13) He wants the church to represent Christ, who, in turn, is "the radiance of God's glory and the exact representation of His being." (Hebrews 1:3) This requires more than our will-power—it can be accomplished only through God-power.

If there is a power outage in the church, we have no one to blame but ourselves. God does not make His power available to those who:

* ✦ Do not believe. (Matthew 13:58)
* ✦ Do not ask. (James 4:2)
* ✦ Ask for the wrong reasons. (James 4:3)

However, He is more than willing and able to empower those who set their hearts:

* ✦ To believe. (Ephesians 1:18)
* ✦ To bless people. (Matthew 14:14)
* ✦ To be witnesses. (Acts 1:8)
* ✦ To bring Him glory. (John 11:4)

A life of worship is one of constantly drawing near to God. It centers us in His will and His purposes for our lives, opening the way for His power to flow through us. It is the only way to bring Him pleasure.

*F*REE TO WORSHIP

We have a choice, just like Israel did after God set them free from Egyptian captivity. He called them to worship.

They chose to turn away. He called them to a feast in His honor. They chose to have a party in honor of a golden calf.

Our worship consists not of what we do or do not do, but how we live our lives. (Romans 12: 1) It's what happens when we live in relationship with the Father. When we live close to Him, we can hear His voice. When He tells us what to do and we do it, He gets the glory.

Worship and Revelation

There can be no worship without revelation. This revelation has two parts. The first part is seeing just how great and glorious God is. The second part is recognizing and releasing from within us whatever gifts He has deposited there.

This is beautifully illustrated in the life of Isaiah:

> In the year that King Uzziah died, I saw the Lord, high and exalted, seated on a throne; and the train of his robe filled the temple. Above him were seraphim, each with six wings: with two wings they covered their faces, with two they covered their feet, and with two they were flying. And they were calling to one another: "Holy, holy, holy is the Lord God Almighty; the whole earth is full of his glory." At the sound of their voices the doorposts and threshholds shook and the temple was filled with smoke. "Woe to me!" I cried. "I am ruined! For I am a man of unclean lips, and I live among a people of unclean lips, and my eyes have seen the King, the Lord Almighty." Then one of the seraphim flew to me with a live coal in his hand, which he had taken with tongs from the altar. With it he touched my mouth and said, "See, this has touched your lips; your guilt is taken away and your sin atoned for." Then I heard the voice of the Lord saying,

"Whom shall I send? And who will go for us?" And I
said, "Here am I. Send me!" (Isaiah 6:1-8)

The presence of the Lord is so wonderful and fearsome
that no human can bear to be there, yet it is so wonderful
and awesome that no one would ever want to leave. In His
presence Isaiah saw and heard. This is not an everyday seeing
and hearing, it is the kind that changes a person. It makes
human agendas fade away. Suddenly, nothing matters but the
greatness of God and the joy of pleasing Him.

There is no place for pride in His presence. When Isaiah saw
the Lord, he was undone. Nothing within him was worthy,
and he knew it. Nothing in him could even begin to compare
with the glory of the Lord. He expressed this condition by
saying, "Woe is me, for I am a man of unclean lips and I live
among a people of unclean lips." (Isaiah 6:5)

Coming into the presence of the Lord makes us aware of
our sin like nothing else can. That is probably why so few
people want to do it. But God doesn't reveal our sin to rub
our faces in it. He does it because He has the only remedy.
Only He can cleanse us. Only He can transform us. Only He
can show us who we were meant to be.

CREATED TO WORSHIP

God wants us to meet with Him because He created us to
worship Him. In His presence we discover who we are and
are given the power to become what we are not yet.

The Holy Spirit is God's change agent:

Now the Lord is the Spirit, and where the Spirit of the
Lord is, there is freedom. And we all, who with unveiled
faces contemplate the Lord's glory are being transformed

into his image with ever-increasing glory, which comes from the Lord, who is the Spirit."(2 Corinthians 3:17-18)

As we behold His glory, we are transformed. As we are transformed, we come to behave more and more like the Father. We reflect His glory.

The English Standard Version says we are changed "from one degree of glory to another." This can be a slow process. It might very well take more than one trip.

We can't change without the power of the Holy Spirit. We can't love people because we read about love in God's rule book. It's not like we make a decision, flip a switch, and suddenly become more loving.

We love people because we are sons and daughters of the kindest, most loving being in existence. We learn how to love because we are being shaped by Him, and He is love. Love becomes who we are, not what we are supposed to do.

God wants to show us the way. It is a way to relate to Him that reveals, in turn, the way we should walk. It is a way of freedom, worship, and walking as sons and daughters of God Most High. It's the way of coming into His presence and being transformed from one degree of glory to another.

THE CENTER OF GOD'S WILL

Going back to the analogy of building a highway, let's suppose everything is built and we are almost ready to open it up. The only thing missing is the center stripe. What would it look like?

The writer of Hebrews tells us, "Consequently, when Christ came into the world, he said … 'I have come to do your will, O God.'" (Hebrews 10:5, 7) The night before His crucifixion He prayed in the garden, "Father, if you are willing, remove this cup from me. Nevertheless, not my will, but yours be done." (Luke 22:42) Therefore, we could say Jesus began and ended His ministry with basically the same goal in mind. His life from beginning to end was about doing the will of the Father.

Long before Jesus came to show us the way, the Father willed for Him to do so. There is a way because first there was a will.

If we don't know God's will, we can't do it. The Bible can tell us the general will of God, but only the Holy Spirit can tell us His specific will for a given place and time. Those who tell us this is no longer possible are reducing the Bible to a book of facts rather than a book of truth.

"Who then, are those who fear the Lord? He will instruct them in the ways they should choose." (Psalm 25:12) Our way is chosen for us by God, not by chance or circumstances.

The Bible clearly states that it not out of reach for common Christians to know God's will. In fact, we are commanded to. Ephesians tells us to "find out what pleases the Lord." (Ephesians 5:10) It goes on to say:

> Be very careful, then, how you live—not as unwise but as wise, making the most of every opportunity, because the days are evil. Therefore do not be foolish, but understand what the Lord's will is. Do not get drunk on wine, which leads to debauchery. Instead, be filled with the Spirit." (Ephesians 5:15-18)

By knowing and doing His will, we can bring pleasure to God:

> Therefore, I urge you, brothers and sisters, in view of God's mercy, to offer your bodies as a living sacrifice,

holy and pleasing to God—this is your true and proper worship.

Do not conform to the pattern of this world, but be transformed by the renewing of your mind. Then you will be able to test and approve what God's will is—his good, pleasing, and perfect will." (Romans 12:1-2)

The center stripe of our highway is the will of God. As long as we allow ourselves to be directed by Him, we will walk in a way that brings pleasure to our Father. This is where we can be confident that He will release His grace and power for our good and for the benefit of those we serve.

How good would it feel to know you were living a life that pleased the Father and brought a smile to His face? This is our purpose, it is our hope, it is our joy—only in this will we find true fulfillment. We can find guidelines for pleasing God in the Bible, but only through obedience to the Holy Spirit can we experience the pleasure of participating in God's will.

When we always say, "God, would you please do something for me?" we are living pineapple upside-down-cake lives. Delicious, but not healthy. The essential question we should be asking is, "How can I please You?" This is our purpose, this is our passion, and it is the surest way to be led to action that has eternal value.

* ✦ *

CHAPTER 15

IF IT'S BROKEN DON'T FIX IT

I live in a high and holy place, but also with the one

who is contrite and lowly in spirit....

ISAIAH 57:15

The Pharisees loved the law because it gave them power. They were proud and unbroken, and that was their downfall. It's the reason they were always in conflict with Jesus.

We are called to walk in the Spirit so that the power of God can be released for the benefit of the people around us.

We should never be proud of being used by God. He was able to use a mule to talk to Balaam. He could do it without us, but it is His great pleasure to include us in seeing His will done on earth as it is in heaven.

THE RIGHT TOOLS FOR THE JOB

There is one part of Gideon's story I have not yet covered. Interestingly enough, it's the climax—the part where doing something God's way worked and produced the results everyone was looking for.

Gideon and his tiny "army" of 300 men had one chal-
lenge—how to defeat a Midianite hoard of many thousands.
Fortunately, God told them how to do it.

The first part of most jobs involves picking the right tools.
In war, if all else is more or less equal, the side with the best
weapons used in the right way wins. But God didn't even tell
them to use weapons. The tools God told them to use were
trumpets, jars, and torches. These are not the things I would
have chosen.

Then there was the strategy. Put the torches in the jars.
Station yourselves around the enemy. Break the jars. Blow the
trumpets. End of plan. And there was no plan B.

Of course the strategy worked. The Midianites, convinced
they were surrounded, were thrown into panic and confusion.
The Lord caused the warriors in the camp to fight each other
with their swords. Those who were not killed fled and were
hotly pursued by the Israelites. Victory was achieved with the
most unlikely of weapons.

Let's look at Gideon's weapons a little more closely:

+ The trumpets represent standing in unity. One sound. One
goal. One Spirit.

+ The torches represent the fire of passion. Doing that thing
you know in your heart God has called you to do.

+ The jars with the torches in them represent us. The glory of
God in us. Treasure in jars of clay. The jars concealed the
light until the proper moment. Then they had to be broken.[1]

*B*ROKENNESS

Perhaps the most amazing thing about Christianity is that

---

1   David Estes, *Warrior, Builder, Dreamer*, LifeAustin Church, July 15, 2013.

God has chosen to reveal His glory through broken people. "We are his body—his hands, feet, voice—and what he does, he'll do through us. We're Plan A and there is no Plan B."[2]

It's a daunting thought that we are called to do the will of God as revealed to us by the Holy Spirit, when He says to do it and in the way that He would do it. It sounds hard, but it doesn't have to be. We are the ones who make it difficult.

We live in a culture that moves farther and farther away every day from the character traits required to live in this manner. That should not surprise us. The things of this world always oppose the ways of God. The flow of the world's current is always contrary to the flow of the Holy Spirit.

"Don't be selfish; don't try to impress others. Be humble, thinking of others as better than yourselves. Don't look out only for your own interests, but take an interest in others, too." (Philippians 2:3-4, NLT)

The culture we're living in is traveling down the wrong track. One that promotes independence, competition, pride, and even greed. Perhaps we need to change trains.

It all boils down to one question. How badly do we want transformation?

The passage in Philippians goes on:

> You must have the same attitude that Christ Jesus had. Though he was God, he did not think of equality with God as something to cling to. Instead, he gave up his divine privileges; he took the humble position of a slave [servant] and was born as a human being. When he appeared in human form, he humbled himself in obedience to God and died a criminal's death on a cross. (Philippians 2:5-8, NLT)

2 Sheets, *Watchman Prayer*, p. 92.

Several words and phrases here are keys to being like Jesus—and being transformed. They are about our attitude. Jesus gave up His privileges. He became a servant. He obeyed. These are not the things most Americans find worthy of pursuit.

Jesus promised that if He was lifted up, all men would be drawn to Him. I'm not sure what we are lifting up in many of our churches, but it must not be Jesus. People desperate for the powerful touch of Christ would tear the roof off a house to get to Him but will not darken the door of a church building where His presence is lacking.[3]

I'm pretty sure that when Jesus said, "If I be lifted up," He was referring to the cross. He was lifted up in brokenness. In His own words, "This is my body, broken for you." It was in that moment that things began to turn. In that instant of brokenness and death, the curtain was torn.

It was because of His willingness to be broken that God exalted Him. "Therefore God exalted him to the highest place and gave him the name that is above every name, that at the name of Jesus every knee should bow, in heaven and on earth and under the earth, and every tongue acknowledge that Jesus Christ is Lord, to the glory of God the Father." (Philippians 2:9-11)

Therefore—because of, as a result of, stemming directly from the fact that He humbled himself, became a servant, obeyed, and was broken on the cross—God raised Him from the dead and seated Him at His own right hand.

---

3 Eldredge, *The Journey of Desire,* p. 39.

God Wants No Less from Us

"My sacrifice, O God is a broken spirit; a broken and contrite heart you, God, will not despise." (Psalm 51:17) Our sacrifice, our worship is to bring God our brokenness and make ourselves available for Him to use.

Here is how I think of it. One day God gives me a beautiful pane of blue glass to carry. I want to please Him, so I carry it until I fall and, inevitably, break it. I get up, and with tears in my eyes, I humbly bring Him the broken pieces. He smiles, takes them from me, and gives me a beautiful pane of red glass, which I carry until I fall and break it. This goes on for many days and with many different colors of glass.

Finally, one day after I hand over the broken pieces of the yellow glass He gave me and get another blue pane, I start to walk away, but then I turn around to ask Him why He still trusts me, why He keeps on giving me new glass, no matter how many times I fall.

Then I see He has taken my many-colored pieces of broken glass and formed them into a beautiful and radiant stained-glass window. I stand amazed.

He smiles at me again and proudly says, "Look at this. This is the life story of my servant. Isn't it beautiful?"

That's what a redeemer does.

God's Dwelling Place

"For this is what the high and exalted One says—He who lives forever, whose name is holy: 'I live in a high and holy place, but also with the one who is contrite and lowly in spirit, to revive the spirit of the lowly and to revive the heart of the contrite." (Isaiah 57:15)

I am so thankful for this passage of scripture.

Our brokenness is precious to Him. In humility we come into His presence where we can see Him as He is and worship Him. His presence, in turn, reveals our brokenness. It shows us we can be transformed only in His power. We are utterly dependent on His goodness and grace.

Nothing else can set us free from our pride, selfishness, and misguided agendas. These stand in direct opposition to true worship.

Worship is a continual turning to God in brokenness, humility, and availability. Worship produces hope, expectancy, vision, motivation, and joy. It makes way for a humble lifestyle that is open to God's input and adjustment. It also opens the way for the power of God to operate in our lives.

Brokenness makes us teachable. We listen best when it becomes obvious that our ways cannot see us through. Our strength is not enough, and our coping mechanisms are like straw that instantly curls up and disappears in the furnace.

His strength is made perfect in our weakness, but our brokenness also positions us to touch others in theirs. Our oldest daughter was killed in an automobile accident in 2010. She was 32 years old. It was an extremely difficult thing to go through. Yes, it still brings me great sadness, but it has also changed the way I see God, heaven, and people.

In our places of greatest brokenness we learn what we really believe about God. When everything else is stripped away, the one thing I know is that God is faithful. Many times that was the only way I was able to face the day—the only way I could continue to put one foot in front of the other and walk on.

A few weeks ago I had the opportunity to visit with a woman who had lost her daughter to cancer a short time before we met. I could speak to her from a place few people know. From that place I could serve her. She had so many questions. I gave her honest answers. I think I helped her a little. That's what we are supposed to do.

GRATITUDE

Have you ever noticed that humble people are also grateful people? When we realize the extent to which we need God, we become extra thankful for all His benefits.

When I was young, my favorite holiday was Christmas, because it was all about me and what I would receive. Later, when I had young children of my own, it was probably still my favorite, but for a different reason. I loved the joy of giving and of seeing the faces of my children light up with delight as they opened each new present.

Finally, I began to be uncomfortable with the commercialization, the money spent, and the frequent feeling of emptiness when the actual occasion failed to live up to the hype. A new favorite holiday emerged. It's Thanksgiving.

I like Thanksgiving because it's Christmas without the hype. It's about getting together as a family and enjoying good food and good fellowship. It's about being grateful and just hanging out. It's a feast and a form of communion.

Giving thanks is good for the soul. Show me a person who can be thankful no matter what their circumstances are, and I will show you a person who understands worship—a person close to God's own heart.

I wonder if Thanksgiving might be God's favorite holiday, too. He has always been a big fan of feasts, fellowship, and faith. I think most of us would be amazed at just how much He likes to be with us. But we shouldn't be.

The evidence is seen throughout scripture. The design of the tabernacle. The grain, the new wine, and the oil. The water He turned to wine. The feast declared when the prodigal son returned. The gift of His son, Jesus Christ.

The evidence is also within us. Eternity set within our hearts. The joy of praise and worship. The gift of the Holy Spirit—the Spirit of adoption.

He gives us such good gifts.

*T*HE GIFTS ARE FOR SERVING

Jesus took the form of a servant. He left us an example that we should do the same. Servants realize that God has given us gifts not so that we can consume them upon ourselves. Rather, they are for serving one another.

"Now to each one the manifestation of the Spirit is given for the common good." (1 Corinthians 12:7)

I believe that so much of what is amiss in the church stems from Christians who want God to serve them. They want Him to fix all their problems and make their lives smooth and prosperous. It's the idea of church as a country club, and it's completely out of touch with living lives that matter.

"There are different kinds of gifts, but the same Spirit distributes them. There are different kinds of service, but the same Lord. And there are different kinds of working, but in all of them and in everyone, it is the same God at work." (1 Corinthians 12:4-6)

Father, Son, and Holy Spirit. It takes all three members of the Trinity for the fullness of God to be expressed in the church.

Nine gifts are listed in 1 Corinthians.

> For to one is given the word of wisdom through the Spirit, to another the word of knowledge through the same Spirit, to another faith by the same Spirit, to another gifts of healings by the same Spirit, to another the working of miracles, to another prophecy, to another discerning of spirits, to another different kinds of tongues, to another the interpretation of tongues. But one and the same Spirit works all these things, distributing to each one individually as He wills. (1 Corinthians 12:8-11, NKJV)

I have found that I tend to function in one or two of these gifts more often than I do in others. As a result, I tend to have more faith in those areas. However, any Christian can function in any gift at any given time, because they are distributed *as He wills*, on the basis of what is needed at the moment.

The gifts of the Holy Spirit are part of our promise land. The gifts in you are for me and the gifts in me are for you. They are our inheritance in the saints. (Ephesians 1:18)

Making a difference is about being in touch with, and being guided by, the Holy Spirit. Jesus did only what He saw the Father doing. Imagine what kind of impact the church could have on the world if we lived by the same principle. When we know the Father, we know His ways. If we always walk with Him, we will never stray from His path. If we know what He would do, we automatically know what we should do.

If God lives in us through the gift of the Holy Spirit, we can hear His voice internally. He can guide us in His ways. He will lead us from the middle of nowhere to the center of God's will.

*M*R. AMERICA

What does it look like to be guided by the Holy Spirit? Let's consider some examples.

Robert Morris, pastor of Gateway Church in Southlake, Texas, tells of an event that happened one day when he and his wife were dining in a cafeteria-style restaurant. A muscular man and his wife came in and sat down. Robert's gaze was drawn to the man, and he felt like he had a word for him.

This impression continued until Robert got up and approached the couple's table. He broke the ice by asking if the man had ever lifted weights. After a chuckle, the man responded that yes, he had done so a time or two (he was a former Mr. America).

Robert then asked if he might share something with the man that he felt like he had heard from God. The man said, "Yes" and invited Robert to sit down.

Robert told the man that he saw him as a child, sitting on his grandmother's lap, crying. His grandmother told him that if he would give his life to the Lord, he would make him strong like Samson. Robert saw that he had made that commitment. His word for the man was that God had made him strong, but he had not fulfilled his part of the deal.

The man looked blankly back at Robert for long enough to cause Robert to fear he had "missed it." Then the man began to cry and looked at his wife, who was also crying.

The man informed Robert that he had just told his wife that story. He knew he had not completed his part of the deal but really didn't know how to approach God. Robert then led both of them to the Lord.[4]

---

4   Robert Morris, *The God I Never Knew* (Colorado Springs, CO: Waterbrook Press, 2011), pp. 123-124.

Several elements of this story are important to consider. The first is that this happened in the course of normal life. Robert was not out looking for someone to evangelize.

Second, note how Robert received the word. It came into his mind as both a picture and as words. These could not have been from Robert, because he had never seen the man before.

Third, the timing could have come only from the Holy Spirit. The man had just told his wife the story in the car on the way to eat.

REINCARNATION?

One day at work, two of my fellow firefighters were having a discussion about reincarnation. After a while, one of them looked up and asked me if there was anything in the Bible that disagreed with the concept.

I had never really thought about it, but a verse of scripture immediately came to mind. I replied that the Bible says, "It is appointed unto man once to die, and after that the judgment." (Hebrews 9:27) For a moment the room got very quiet.

We can trust the Holy Spirit to bring to mind the right words at the right time for a given situation.

ON THE ROAD AGAIN

A woman had a grown-up son who drove a tractor-trailer rig for a living. One night she was awakened from sleep four times. Each time she "saw" in her mind her son's truck going off the road. Each time she prayed for her son's safety until she had peace about it, and then went back to sleep.

The next day her son called. He told her his truck had almost gone off the road four times during the night and asked her if she had been praying.[5]

---

5   Sheets, *Watchman Prayer,* pp. 74-75.

Something similar often happened to my wife and me while our children were teenagers. One of us would be awakened at night to pray. We didn't always find out why, but there is no doubt in my mind that God woke us up to pray them through situations where either their bodies or their spirits needed protection.

A HEALING

For many years my wife worked as an operating room nurse. One day while positioning a patient for surgery, she felt led to pray for his healing, so she did. A few minutes later the doctor opened the patient's chest, looking to remove a baseball-sized tumor. But there was no tumor there.

*G*OD IS NOT WEIRD

In none of these examples did anyone get weird. These were just ordinary people in the course of living ordinary lives when God stepped in. No one was overcome. No one lost control. No one made a scene.

God is not weird, and He has no desire to make us weird. That would cause us to represent Him incorrectly. God is supernatural. Big difference.

God is not the author of confusion. (1 Corinthians 14:33 KJV) His intervention in our lives is not meant to cause people to scratch their heads and wonder, "What in the world was that?" The reason He gives us the Holy Spirit is to draw people to Him, not chase them away in horror. As always, God wants to bring people to Himself.

"Every good and perfect gift is from above, coming down from the Father of the heavenly lights, who does not change like shifting shadows." (James 1:17) The gift of the Holy

Spirit is a good and perfect gift from God. He is to be joyfully received, not feared. He will meet us in our brokenness, leading and empowering us to do the will of God by serving one another. He is our inheritance in the saints.

There was nothing special about the people God used in the examples above. We were used by God because we were available. I know that I have missed opportunities to be used by God sometimes. I felt a prompting to do something but let the opportunity pass or talked myself out of it. Other times I have been right on target. John Ortberg calls this being willing to turn aside, like Moses did to investigate the burning bush. He let God interrupt the normal flow of his day. Had he not, "he would have just missed the Exodus, the people of Israel, his calling, the reason for his existence. He would have missed knowing God."[6]

THE CENTER OF GOD'S WILL

What would it look like to live in the center of God's will? Would God speak to us every minute of every day, telling us where to go, where to park, and how to minister to people all the time? It hasn't worked that way for me and probably not for anyone else, either.

It was the apostle Paul who saw the need for the Spirit of wisdom and revelation, hope, inheritance, and power so that we can know God better and do stuff in His name and for His glory. But even the apostle Paul, while on his missionary journeys, spent time making tents.

I think God knows how to keep us grounded. He wants us to have one foot in reality and one foot in His kingdom. We are the intersection of heaven and earth.

---

6   John Ortberg, *The Life You've Always Wanted*, p.18.

Think about it. Even Jesus spent a lot of time just walking. Maybe that's when He listened. Today the pace is so fast and our schedules are so packed that listening takes effort. It doesn't come naturally. It's a choice that we either make or fail to make every day.

God loves for us to seek Him. As we worship Him, we turn our hearts toward Him. We develop listening ears. Then we are able to hear Him when He speaks. We are not bothered when He interrupts our day to give us an assignment.

As I said earlier, we are plan A. "Plan B is to waste the cross; to leave the tormented in their torment; to scream with our silence. 'There is no hope'; to hear the Father say again, 'I looked, but found no one....'"[7]

*H*E Is

I pray this book has encouraged you to believe that *God is*, and that He is a rewarder of those who diligently seek Him. Because He is, and He is.

I also hope this book has raised more questions than it has answered. It was not my purpose to answer questions, but to point to the way, the truth, and the life. As we learn to listen and obey God's will, what He speaks to you will be very different than what He speaks to me.

Only the sum total of our giftings will reflect the glory of Christ like the many facets of a beautiful diamond. The church will only magnify the Lord as each part does its work. I need you, because God's gifts in you are my inheritance. Only together can we become His fullness.

---

7   Dutch Sheets, *Intercessory Prayer* (Ventura, CA: Regal Books, 1996), p 48.

"Come to me with your ears wide open. Listen, and you will find life. I will make an everlasting covenant with you.... Seek the Lord while you can find him. Call on him now while he is near." (Isaiah 55:3,6, NLT)

✳ ✳ ✳

ACKNOWLEDGMENTS

To my wife, Carla (who can herd cats). Supporting me and believing in me through the process of writing this book had been more difficult than that, I know. Thank you.

Thanks to Paul Davis, Steve Cundiff, and all the other friends who provided feedback and encouragement along the way. You are all invaluable and irreplaceable parts of my life.

Thank you to the pastors, staff, leaders, and members of LifeAustin Church for helping me see how transformation takes place.

I would be amiss not to acknowledge Frank Ball, leader of my first writer's group, and Leena Nelson Dooley and "the girls" of my second. These wonderful people provided honest feedback and motivation at the same time. They taught me the craft of writing.

Many thanks to TLC Graphics and Narrow Gate Books for providing great graphics, editing, and printing. Specifically, I want to thank Dick Christianson, my editor, for his contributions, and Monica Thomas for the interior design.

Finally, thanks to Tamara Dever, owner of TLC Graphics, who did the beautiful cover design and presided over the rest of the process. You were upbeat, encouraging, and helpful, and you always exceeded my expectations. Thank you.

ABOUT THE AUTHOR

KERRY JOHNSTON is a follower of Jesus, retired Fire Captain, writer, and ordinary guy. His firefighting career spanned 33 years and two fire departments in Texas. He has never been to seminary or held a pastoral position, and writes about spiritual life from his experience in the trenches, his personal walk with the Lord, and out of a deep passion to see the church become all God intended for it to be, one person at a time.

He currently resides in Austin, Texas with his wife Carla and two cats. He is the father of three wonderful children, one of whom has preceded him to heaven.